MW00965312

OUT IN THE GARDEN

month by month advice for
a Cape Cod garden

written & illustrated
by
Martha Hughes
~ master gardener ~

OUT IN THE GARDEN

Invisible Ink Publishing
2 Smith Lane
Brewster, MA 02631

Portions of this book have appeared in
The Cape Cod Chronicle
and The Cape Codder newspapers

back cover photo by Alice Eldridge

ISBN: 1-57502-832-8

Printed in the USA by

MORRIS PUBLISHING
3212 East Highway 30 • Kearney, NE 68847 • 1-800-650-7888

this book is dedicated

with love

to Tom & Lesley

Many thanks to the Barnstable County
Cooperative Extension program:
William Clark and Roberta Clark
(no relation)
As residents of this beautiful and fragile Cape Cod,
we are very fortunate to have an active
Extension service. I truly appreciate the
training and continuing education I receive through
the Master Gardener program.
And thanks also to the three women who answer
all my questions and keep the Extension office
running with cheerful expertise:
Marilyn Clark, Pat Clark, Barbara Clark
(no relation)
just kidding, it's
Marilyn Myers, Pat Weekes, Barbara Conway
the best!

Table of Contents

Introduction

o you love to talk about gardens? Me too. I love to see gardens, work in the garden, learn about gardens, talk about gardens, oh yes, and write about gardens.

Gardens are a great equalizer. I have met so many wonderful, interesting people through gardening. There are many plants-people here on Cape Cod. Some are extreme gardeners with gardening as raison d' etre, "I garden, therefore I am". There are window-sill gardeners, people with one tomato in a pot. And there are the rest of us who are somewhere in between.

Do you think of the word "garden" as a noun or a verb? "I have a garden," or "I garden on Cape Cod". Have you noticed that gardeners are tossing around the Latin names for plants more often? I like to use the Latin botanical classification to be specific, not pretentious. Using common names for plants is like using nicknames for friends. When we are looking for a particular plant, it is useful to be exact. If you say you want a *daisy* , you could end up with any of the hundreds of daisy-shaped flowers in many sizes and colors from numerous plant families.

Botanical Latin is a system for classifying and naming, based on the structural similarities in plants. If you read plant labels at the garden center or in catalogues, you'll see that the Latin names consist of at least two words. The first word is the genus (family category) name for the plant. The second, and sometimes third word are adjectives or descriptive words to convey something like color or size. After these words there might be another word or name in single quotes which refers to hybridization. There, have you got it? Garden Latin defined in a paragraph.

Gardening for me is broken down into two groups. There is *head gardening* and *hand gardening* . Head gardening includes my imaginary gardens, book gardens, visiting gardens and other clean hand plant activities. Hand gardening is basically getting out there and doing it. Dirty hands. Hard work. Putting plans into action and learning through doing. Fun!

No two gardens are exactly alike. Plants are living, ever changing organisms. Growing conditions can vary greatly within a small area. A garden can change overnight from a shade garden to an exposed, sunny site by the removal of trees. Or change can be slower as plants mature.

Changes in the Cape Cod weather are what gardeners depend on and curse the most. We need the rain, then we wish it would stop raining. We gamble on those frost dates. We watch that Weather Channel like it's our favorite show.

There is a tremendous variety of plant material from which to choose for any type of garden. New plants are being developed all the time and old varieties are being discovered and brought into the market for us as well. Cape Cod garden centers are carrying more unusual plants every year. There are general and specialty catalogues for mail order. We can even hop onto the internet for plant ordering and information if we have a few hours to spare.

I've been gardening on Cape Cod for almost ten years now and I still feel like I'm just getting started. Before that we lived in Florida and Maine. In Florida we had a cactus garden and citrus and banana trees. In Maine we could grow enormous delphiniums and antique roses. But guess where we grow the best tomatoes? That's right. Cape Cod.

This little book is a gathering of information that I've collected for gardening on Cape Cod. Portions of it have appeared in columns that I've written for the Cape Cod Chronicle and The Cape Codder newspapers.

The Barnstable County Cooperative Extension service is a wonderful resource for horticultural information. It has many educational and research programs that benefit all the residents of Cape Cod. If you are a gardening nut and are interested in community service, you can apply for the Master Gardener program. They take applications each fall and new classes start in February.

Gardening for me is an adventure in trial and error. It's a chance to discover and try new plants with lots of enthusiastic blunders. Garden areas can look wonderful in one year and be embarrassing disasters in another. But even after growing plants for many years, I think my favorite part of gardening is the thrill of seeing a newly sprouted seed. Hopeful beginnings. How about you?

Martha Hughes
~ master gardener ~

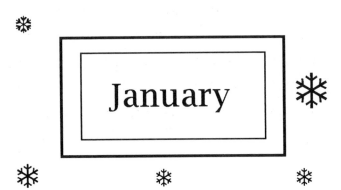

January

January

January in the Cape Cod garden is colored in greens and grays. Whites and beiges. Occasional reds. Subtle blues.

It is the month for the new garden plan. The garden dream is inspired by the riots of color in the plant catalogues that flood the icy mailbox. Is my garden pink and blue this year? Is it orange? Is it purple and forbidden magenta? Which new selection will I not be able to live without? Which old standard will finally find a new home here?

A cautionary note from someone who's done lots of mail order: most plants that you order from a garden catalog will arrive at an inconvenient time, be smaller than you expected and hardly ever perform like the ones in the glossy photos. It's better to cut out the photos (and names) from the catalogues, then take them with you to buy locally in the spring on the day before you have time to plant. There are wonderful nurseries from Provincetown to the Cape Cod Canal where you can find almost every imagined plant for your garden. Some local nurseries will even special order rare and unusual selections for you. And don't forget, May, the plant sale month, is coming too.

Catalogues are still your best choice for buying seeds. The selection is much better than in the stores. Look for new disease resistant varieties of your old favorites. Is this the year you'll try growing something new like easy arugula? White miniature eggplant? Your own red hot chili peppers?

January is a good time to get an X - Ray view of your garden. Look at the bones so to speak. How can you change the skeleton to make it more appealing? Variety! If all your garden shapes are rounded, plan to add something that grows tall and narrow for an exclamation point.

!! ● ▲ ● ▲ ● !!

Try to get away from meatball and upside down ice cream cone plantings around your home. Are all your shrubs in bare stems now? Plan to add some evergreens. Why not try a yellow-green or a blue-green for something different. Is your ground covered with dried up lawn? Plan to add some evergreen ivy or another interesting groundcover.

Indoor Gardening: Pluck up your courage and give that tired ol' houseplant the heave ho. You know,

4

that greenish brown thing on the window sill. Or, if you really can't part with it because, "oh, but I've had it so long, and it really did have a flower on it once", how about re-potting. Buy a slightly bigger pot, maybe something glazed, painted or sculptured. Ignore your instinct to buy a much bigger pot. Buy some good potting soil. It's inexpensive and much better than garden soil for your indoor plants. Add in some slow release fertilizer pellets. If you trim the old roots slightly it will encourage new growth. Clean the leaves unless they are fuzzy (like African violet). Remember to mist with water more often in the winter if the house is dry. Check for any signs of insect pests or mold. Houseplant problems are much easier to treat in early stages. Or pitch that ol' potted brown leafed thing onto the compost and go buy a new houseplant at the nursery or the grocery store.

Outdoors: Keep up the compost. The simplest method of composting is to make a pile of leaves somewhere so they won't all blow away. Then make a shape with a hole in the middle of the top to catch rain water. Add your kitchen scraps (not meat products because they attract vermin), add some seaweed. Toss occasionally. Add some manure - cow, horse, rabbit, goat, chicken, not dog or cat. This is a recipe for black gold - rich, free, organic matter to add to existing flower and vegetable beds or to start new planting areas.

At this time of year, damage can be done to your outside plants by alternate freezing and thawing. Cape Cod can never depend on a constant layer of snow to insulate the garden. When there has been a heavy deep frost on the ground, it is a good time to cover your garden with a mulch of leaves, straw or even the boughs cut from Christmas trees. Oak leaves work well because they do not mat down and rot as quickly as most other fallen leaves. This will hopefully keep the garden soil at a more even temperature so it will not heave and break the plant roots. Plants are weakened by having their cells frozen and unfrozen too quickly. We want our garden to remain dormant, and winter rot kept to a minimum.

Back to pouring over the garden catalogues. The short overcast days and long winter nights of January are filled with gardens imagined, while outside the rhododendron buds are swollen with the promise of spring.

Amaryllis & Snowdrops

Many of us have Amaryllis in bloom now in our homes. The enormous tropical looking blooms make a dramatic display to fight the winter doldrums. I have a garden encyclopedia from 1840 that calls the Amaryllis "eminently ornamental . . . of easy culture; the greatest secret being to give them alternately; a season of excitement and a season of repose." Lovely.

Amaryllis bulbs, *Hippeastrum*, *from hippeus - a knight and astron - a star* grew originally in South America. They were collected and hybridized to get bigger flowers and more variety of color. You can buy bulbs that will have blossoms in reds, pinks, whites, salmons or oranges with combinations of all those colors. They come in single and double blooms. The clue for their care is that they have grown naturally in a climate that is warm and rainy for half the year and dry and cool for the other half.

The Amaryllis is very easy to grow. The trick is getting them to rebloom in another season. Unlike many other flowering houseplants, the size and number of flowers increase each year with the age of the plant.

An Amaryllis blooms best if it is grown in a pot just an inch or so bigger than the bulb. You can also plant three or more bulbs close together in a large pot for a spectacular effect. Plant in potting soil (not garden soil) leaving 1/3 of the bulb above the soil line. Be careful with the fleshy roots because they can break off. Keep moist but not soaked and in a sunny, warm location.

Start the bulbs in the soil about six to eight weeks before the date when you want the blooms to open, but this is not an exact time frame. One year I planted four Amaryllis bulbs at two week intervals to have a succession of bloom throughout the winter. But the bulbs were too slow or too fast and they all bloomed at the same time.

Usually the hollow flower stalks will come up before the leaves. If leaves come up and you wait and wait and wait and no flower stalk comes up, it often means that the pot is too big for the bulb. When the flowers begin to open, move the pot to a cooler place out of direct sun and the blossoms will last much longer - up to a month.

Pinch off the spent blossoms or the plant will use too much energy making seeds. The Amaryllis bulb is a cousin to the daffodil and likewise needs to have its leaves left on after the blossoms go by, to make food reserves for next year's flowers. Continue to water and fertilize until the leaves start to turn yellow. This usually happens in the summer. Then stop watering and turn the pot on it's side so you won't water it by mistake.

Let the plant rest like this for a couple of months. Put it someplace where you won't have to look at it because it starts to look pathetic and you might be tempted to toss it. Cut off the dried leaves. Then you can start all over again next fall for bigger and better flowers in the winter from the same bulb. The Amaryllis can stay in the same pot for up to five years. Just scrape out an inch or so of the soil and put in some fresh potting soil each year.

Outside the first Snowdrops are blooming just above the layer of "poorman's fertilizer" also known as snow. Snowdrops, *Galanthus*, *gala - milk* and *anthos - flower* , are also hardy cousins to the Amaryllis. The fragile nodding appearance of the white and green flowers belies the tough nature of this minor bulb.

The best way to introduce Snowdrops to your yard is to divide a clump from somewhere else when their leaves are starting to turn yellow later in the spring. You can also buy dry bulbs in the fall. There are many named hybrids (difficult to find) but the differences in the flowers are so subtle that you'd have to be down on your knees, with a magnifying glass, outside in winter, to see the difference. We leave that to the fanatics.

Every January I say I'm going to plant more Snowdrop bulbs in the fall. But either I forget or go for the more colorful bulbs that come up later. Maybe this fall I'll remember how much better January is when the snowdrops are blooming. I mean, they're no Superbowl or anything, but they are exciting in a gardener thrill kind of way.

Plans

Winter is a good time to plan for next summer's lower maintenance landscape. Before you get out the graph paper and plan something that would be better suited for someone with a full time gardener, think about what you want to accomplish on your little bit - o' - earth.

Do you love a lawn but hate to mow? Do you want a 300' perennial bed but don't want to weed or dead-head? Do you love to prune? Do you like bugs or hate 'em?

Gardens take time. Some more than others, but every garden needs some maintenance. There's no such thing as a garden in a can. Seeds may come that way, but gardens are work.

Review the environment first before you start to choose plants. The climate or zone, the soil, light and wind exposures, salt, and the topography all play important roles in the ultimate success or failure of the garden.

Cape Cod has many climates from a Truro Tundra to a Brewster Banana Belt. There are even micro climates within your own yard. The sunny side. The windy side. The side that still hasn't recovered since Hurricane Bob came through in '91.

If you're choosing a new site or reviewing an old site for a vegetable garden, the best location is where it gets the most sun. You can adjust the soil, the water and the wind exposure but if you don't get 6 to 8 hours of sun, those vegetable plants just aren't going to produce. Don't plant palm trees outside in Orleans. Don't plant tomatoes in the shade.

Flower gardens can be adjusted to a variety of sites by choosing sun or shade loving plants. Do a little research on the plants you are planning to include in your garden. Marginally hardy plants may survive with some fussing but are you willing to spend that much time on winter protection?

After you know the growing conditions of your property, you can plan the shapes and sizes of your gardens. Straight lines and symmetrical plantings give a formal appearance. Flowing curves are more casual and visually more interesting for a home garden. Try to make the beds narrow so you can work in them without stepping in and compacting the soil.

Take some time this winter to look at the wonderful collection of garden books at the libraries. The bookstores all have garden sections now too. My favorites for armchair garden travel are the big coffee table books with lots of color glossies.

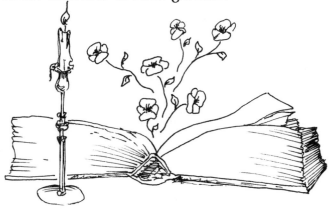

For garden help it's a good idea to check out the garden clubs and plant societies here on Cape Cod. There are many of them for general gardening such as town and community clubs.   Men's garden clubs. Women's garden clubs. Clubs for specific plant groups such as the Rhododendron Society, Orchid Society, Rose Society, Bonsai Club, etc. . . have you noticed that there is a club for every interest on Cape Cod?

Ivies

The elegant and familiar English Ivy is an underutilized plant that does very well both indoors and out on Cape Cod. A member of the Ginseng family, Ivy (Latin - *Hedera*) has a preferred habitat in a shaded woodland where it creeps along the ground sending out roots as it goes. When the plant encounters a tree or other vertical obstruction, it climbs and has been known to reach 100' or more.

Ivy does better if it is not in full sun whether on a window sill or outside. It will survive, but growth will be slower with occasional leaf burn. An evergreen, generally pest and disease free, ivy is a very long lived plant with many examples that are hundreds of years old.

According to research carried out by NASA, the common English Ivy is a good defense against indoor air pollution. Ivy plants clean the air of pollutants including benzene which is a carcinogen present in paints, solvents and cigarette smoke.

Ivy has two life phases: the juvenile and the adult form which is also called also called arborescent stage.

All over Cape Cod you can see the evergreen ivy growing wild on the forest floor and up around tree trunks. The lobed, cut leaf or heart shaped leaves are of the immature stage of the ivy plant and the oval, dark green leaves that you see on woody vines going up trees are the adult stage of the ivy plant. The flower clusters and small black seed pods are on the adult form only. This metamorphosis of leaf shape and stem texture is unusual for the plant kingdom.

English Ivy can be an attractive problem solver in the landscape. At home in a formal or natural setting it softens hard edges quickly. Use ivy to cover an unsightly stump or replace grass on a hard to mow, steep area. It has a natural propensity for self-clinging, but you can assist and encourage better growth by tying ivy to supports. Try to keep any ivy from growing up your favorite trees. It can make a lot of extra weight that 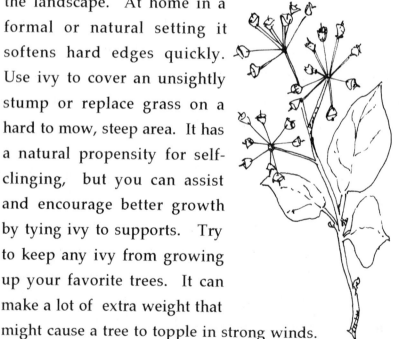 might cause a tree to topple in strong winds.

Good companion plants for ivy are ferns, clematis and hosta. Pansies will last longer in the garden when their roots are shaded by ivy.

Underplant ivy with spring bulbs; the leaves will cover the dying foliage after the bulb flowers have gone by.

Ivy is used both indoors and out for topiary; shaping plants to form living sculpture. For a quick, inexpensive topiary cone for your garden, use an upside down tomato cage for a frame. Affix it down firmly on the ground or in a large pot so it won't blow over. Gather the loose ends together at the top with a wire. If desired, you can add extra support for the ivy by attaching chicken wire or other light weight wire fencing to the tomato cage. Spray paint the form dark green and plant all around the base with a lot of small leaved ivy plants. Try to buy ones that already have long vines. Loosely tie the vines up the form all season until it is covered.

If you plant a topiary in a pot, you can bring it inside to enjoy all winter. Create other shapes with wire to cover with ivy and make your own Museum Of Vine Arts.

Ivy comes in many leaf shapes and colors. 'Goldheart' for example is hardy here and has green leaf edges with a pretty yellow center and red stems. As a houseplant, ivy will tolerate neglect but its greatest enemy is overwatering. It will last a long time as foliage in a cut flower arrangement and it won't wilt when used around the base of candles for a table setting.

There are many Ivy Impostors. German Ivy and Swedish Ivy are not true Ivy but make good house plants. Boston Ivy covers the walls of Harvard Yard but it's not an Ivy either; it is more closely related to Grapes than Ivy. But the most infamous ivy impostor on Cape Cod is *Poison Ivy* .

Poison ivy, *Rhus radicans* is from the Cashew family. I don't have to describe what it looks like, everyone knows poison ivy, "leaves of three, let them be". If it is not avoided or properly controlled, poison ivy can create problems for people from minor skin irritations to burning, infected rashes and fever.

There are currently only two recommended methods for eradicating this noxious plant. One is to pull it up by hand (hopefully covered in a disposable glove) when the soil is moist, be careful to make sure all the roots come out. The other method is to spray with a herbicide when the poison ivy leaves are full out on a warm, sunny day when there is no wind. Read and follow all herbicide labels and directions carefully and make sure that "poison ivy" is listed on the label. The smoke from poison ivy is extremely poisonous.

Poison ivy is not recommended for use in flower arrangements even if it does have attractive fall foliage.

February

Paths

hances are, when you moved into your house, you inherited the paths that move you from one place to another on the property: the path to the front door, the path to the driveway. Maybe you've added gardens or trees, maybe an outbuilding, shed or sitting area. Are the existing paths designed to get you from here to there in the quickest manner possible using straight hard surfaces or do the paths slow you down with a curve or an uneven surface?

A well designed path is irresistible. It invites you to move in a certain direction. A path can determine the character of a garden or even an entire property. When you design a new garden or want to improve an old one, think about the garden paths as well as the garden plants. If you want to change, improve or create new pathways there are many things to think about and many path materials from which to choose.

Take a look at any path on your property. Now imagine it with a different surface material - cut stone pavers, pine needles, loose gravel, a grassy strip and since this is Cape Cod, how about crushed shells. Now imagine the same pathway shaped into an *s* - curve or a long curved sweep that is edged with ornamental grasses, fragrant herbs, low growing roses or colorful annuals.

Is there a clearly established path to your house for people to get to the door that you want them to use? The front walkway is a good place for specimen plants that invite close viewing. Move that pathetic, scraggly old shrub to the back of the property where visitors won't see it. Replace it with something that is flowering and fragrant.

Different pathways create varying kinds of movement through your property. Straight, narrow paths tend to quicken the pace because the walker does not have to pay as much attention. Meandering paths encourage slower movement. The path that drastically slows movement is stepping stones or a very rough surface that the walker has to negotiate carefully.

Most paths out in nature are not straight. Animal trails twist and turn through the woods. When people make paths through fields or across a grassy area, they are seldom in straight lines when seen from a birds eye view. But sometimes we want a straight path. It may be the shortest way to the mailbox. A straight path might be needed to tie together two architectural features. Or maybe your personality just prefers the straight and narrow. So go ahead and make a straight and narrow path, just remember to make it wide enough for at least two people or a wheelbarrow to get through.

The choices and availability for path materials are great. You can buy natural and manmade path material. Some of the garden centers are carrying path materials now. They can also be purchased at the lumber yards, masonry supply centers, or through landscapers. The library and book stores have instructions for the do-it-yourselfer if you want to try making you own pathways.

Materials for paths are usually broken into two groups - hard and soft. Hard material includes such things as natural stones, concrete, bricks, and crushed stone. Soft materials can include mulches, pine needles, moss, grass, seaweed or other organic matter.

Here are some short definitions for a few path materials so you'll know what to ask about:

AGGREGATE are small loose stones,

COBBLESTONES are cut granite cubes generally
    10 x 4 x 4 inches,

CUT STONE is natural stone cut into rectangles
    and squares such as bluestone
    pavers,

FIELDSTONE is naturally occurring, randomly
    shaped stone that is flat on at least
    one side,

FLAGSTONE is usually geometrically shaped and
flat on both sides,
RIVERSTONE is smoothed and rounded over
time by water wearing down the
rough edges - it comes from pea size
to large rocks,
SLATE is quarried and comes in a variety of
thicknesses - it can be slippery
when wet.
And then there are
BRICKS everyone knows what bricks are, you can
buy new or used ones.

You would be amazed by all the patterns that you can
make using bricks or a combination of brick and stone
for a path. There are lots of other materials to choose
from, but these can get you started, on the right path as it
were.

In A Name

Flowers have always been used to express sentiment from one person to another. Today there is a huge industry dedicated to that achievement. Flowers help you to say, "I love you" or "I'm very sorry" or "thank you", "I miss you", "well done", "I'm trying to butter you up", etcetera.

Valentine's Day is a special day set aside to recognize LOVE and express it. You know . . . ROMANCE . . . cards, chocolate and flowers. It's easy to love flowers. They bring beauty, color and fragrance into our lives. I admit it, I'm dazzled by their appeal.

Many of our familiar flowers have interesting histories. The current inventory of plants that we combine freely in our gardens was discovered and collected from places all over the world. There are still plant hunters who search wild places for new species. I know a Rhododendron plant hunter who has collected seed from the wilds of Borneo and Nepal.

Columbus set off into uncharted seas to find the spices and plant treasures of the Indies, not to discover new lands. He didn't send back spices from India, but he and his followers did introduce corn, sweet potatoes, beans, garden peppers and pineapples to Europe. Today, our Space Explor- ation programs might have more financial backing if it was discovered that there was something good to eat out there in the universe.

From Chinese expeditions came forsythia, peony, hollyhocks and chrysanthemum. Japan gave us bleeding hearts and wisteria. Tulips originally came from Turkey. Impatiens and gladiolus came from Africa. Dahlias came from Mexico as did zinnias and cosmos.

The common names of flowers have their origins in folklore from a time before there was scientific classification. Many of these charming names persist to our present day language. How can you resist a flower name like cupid's dart, red hot poker, baby's breath, angel's fishing rod, jewelweed, moonflower, or honesty?

Then there are the flower names that evoke comical images of clothing: dutchman's breeches, lady slippers, bachelor's buttons, Quaker bonnets, Queen Anne's lace, and monk's hoods.

The humble wild pansy that seeds itself all over the garden is known by many names:Johnny - jump -up, heartsease, kiss - her - in - the - buttery, cuddle me, or love - in - idleness.

It would be difficult to find anyone today who did not know the Rose (by any name). It is the most loved of all our cultivated plants.

If you are lucky enough to receive roses for Valentine's Day, here are a few tips to make them last a little longer:

~ Recut the stems with a sharp knife (not serrated edge, not scissors).

~ Place the roses in a container filled with half tepid to cool water and half ginger ale.

~ Add just a drop of bleach to help kill bacteria. Keep in a cool location out of direct sun.

~ Repeat the stem cuts with clean water every day for the longest time of beauty.

~ Keep roses away from drafts and don't place on top of the television.

~ Make sure your roses are not out of the water for very long.

~ Don't drive around with them in your car all day 1/2 hour max.

~ Keep roses away from fresh fruit, and better yet, out of the kitchen.

On February 14th, you can have mushy cards, too much chocolate, plenty of romance, but you can never have enough flowers. Happy Valentine's Day from Sweet William, Sweet Cicely, Rose of Sharon, Pretty Betsy, Busy Lizzie, Herb Robert, Blue-eyed Mary, Black-eyed Susan, Bouncing Bet, Jack - in - the - Pulpit, Stinking Benjamin, Violet, Rose, Althea, Daisey and me . . . Martha.

Begonia

f you say it slowly, the word "begonia" rolls off the tongue with a syrupy drawl - like "magnolia" or "azalea" or "y'all". I picture begonia blossoms lighting up a shady garden in Charleston, a parasol leaning against a crepe myrtle.

The Begonia family is a very large one with great variety of plant form. The Cape Cod grower can find a begonia for use as a houseplant, in a summer window box or flower bed. Some begonias are grown for their flowers and some are grown for their interesting and beautiful leaves. True begonia enthusiasts will pale at the simplification, but I'll try to pass along some general information for the appreciation and care of this plant.

We can divide the begonia family into four branches:

The *semperflorens* group (everflowering) has a fibrous root system and a very long bloom time. This group includes the wax begonia that will be in every garden center this spring. It's a desirable annual bedding plant with red, pink or white flowers that will last all summer. The leaves are green, bronze or red tinted. The wax begonia also makes a good flowering house plant, or a windowbox plant for outside.

The *Rex* group is grown for it's beautiful leaves with jewel colors - amethyst, ruby, aquamarine, opal, pearl, and precious metal shades of gold, silver and bronze. All the Rex begonias can be traced back to a single leaf found growing in the pot of an orchid plant imported into England in the 1800's. This plant has a dormant time when the foliage droops then dies while the plant rests for a season before sending up fresh foliage. Many people think the plant is dead and toss it.

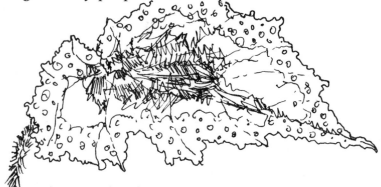

The *angel wing* group, generally grown as a house plant, has the unusual leaf shape described by it's name. The flowers are not as showy, and sometimes are completely hidden. Angel wing begonias come in very small and enormously large leaf varieties. These plants can grow very tall.

Now is a good time to make cuttings of this easily rooted plant. Try to find a branched stem for a cutting so it will have the capacity to branch as a new plant. If you can only make cuttings of stems with no branching, the new plants will be straight and leggy. Try planting multiple cuttings in one pot for the appearance of a bushy plant. You can root the cuttings in sand or sterile potting soil, but I've found it to be easier to stick the cuttings in a glass of water and then plant the cuttings in soil when the roots are about an inch long. The angel wing is a tough plant that doesn't need pampering. I have one that has taken over an East window.

The fourth and most dramatic group is the *tuberous begonia* , grown for it's magnificent, long lasting flowers. Now is a good time to order for next summer's bloom. Modern hybrids are more sturdy with bigger flowers and longer bloom time. The tubers can be planted inside for earlier bloom, but some people wait and plant outside at the same time that it's safe for the tomatoes to go out. All begonias are of tropical origin and will be killed by frost.

For the biggest flowers, it's a good idea to disbud the tuberous begonia. This is when you pinch off some flowers in the bud stage on each stem so the plant can give more energy to fewer flowers. Plant the tubers concave side up near the surface of a well drained, loose soil mixed with peat moss and compost. Fertilize with either water soluble or slow release fertilizer.

When the tuberous begonia plants start to slow down in the fall, cut off the stems and place the roots in paper bags with some peat moss and save for next year. Store in a cool dry place like the cellar if it's not too warm. These plants can also be propagated by rooted stem cuttings. Be sure to make cuttings from leaf stems that do not have blossoms.

For the begonia used as a houseplant, the main cause of death is OVERWATERING. The second-most fatal cause is an environment that is too warm and dry, and whose house isn't, in the winter. Increase the humidity around the houseplant by placing the pot on a dish or tray that has pebbles just covered with water.

All houseplants, including begonias, should be examined at the place of purchase for evidence of insects or disease. It only takes a second to lift up the leaves and look for bugs or mildew before you get the plant home and have to treat the problems. There are thousands of begonias to choose from and one is probably just right for you.

Seeds

Do you think having a big load of cow or horse manure in the back of your car is a good thing? Would you be happy if someone gave you a Chinese food container filled with earthworms? Do you smile when you see bees on all your blossoms? Does your heart skip a beat when you see an ad for a plant sale? If you answered "YES!" to these questions you're a gardener. But you already knew that.

Have you started any seeds yet? Some of my fanatical gardener friends have started tomato seeds already for the earliest fruit but I'm going to wait for a few more weeks.

Now is a good time to plan for disease and pest prevention for next summer's tomatoes. The best way to start is to buy new seed. You can save the seed from a tomato that looks and tastes "perfect", but it is unlikely that you'll be able to reproduce that same fruit from it's seed. If the parent tomato plant was a hybrid, as are most of the ones that we buy, then the offspring may be something quite different.

Look for fresh seed packed for this year. You can plant seeds left over from last year or earlier, but the germination rate will be much lower. Seeds do not stay viable forever unless you store them in a nice, dry ancient pyramid.

I always have seeds left over from one year to the next, it's so hard to throw them out. It seems like there's always extra tomato seeds and never enough morning glory or nasturtium seeds in a package.

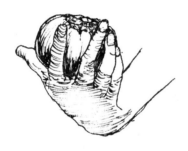

When you buy tomato seeds, look for disease resistant varieties. The easiest way to find this is to look for the letters "V,F,N and T" after the tomato hybrid names in the catalog or on the seed packages. The more of these letters after the name the better. The "V" and "F" stand for Verticillium and Fusarium Wilt resistance. These are fungal diseases that strike many Cape Cod gardens. The "N" stands for nematodes, and the "T" for Tobacco Mosaic resistance.

If you had tomato plants last year that had leaves that wilted, spotted, turned yellow and fell off from the bottom up, it probably was due to Verticillium or Fusarium Wilt. Unfortunately, these are diseases that can persist in the soil for years and even get worse. Don't put the tomatoes in the same place year after year. The best remedy for these problems is prevention.

In the last few years, many of the seed borne diseases have been eliminated. The new tomato seeds available for the home grower have a much better chance for success. Now if they could only develop a good tasting, red tomato that we could grow inside, on the window sill in the winter.

After you find the disease resistance letters, look to see if the tomato plant will be "determinate" or "indeterminate". Determinates stop growing and producing new flowers for fruit when they reach a certain height. Indeterminate tomato plants continue to grow and make fruit all season. These plants do better with heavy duty staking or sturdy, tall cages.

If you're planning to grow tomatoes in containers, look for "determinate" and "patio" varieties. Yellow and orange tomatoes are generally milder tasting and less acidic. Heirloom varieties such as the sweet, red-purple 'Brandywine' are available and worth trying along with some of your old tomato standards.

Be careful not to grow too many cherry tomato plants. You can end up with billions of rotting cherry tomatoes after you've eaten your fill and your neighbors say, "NO MORE!" One seed catalog has a red and yellow striped cherry tomato called 'Tigerette' that looks very interesting.

To get your tomato plants off to a good start, be sure to use sterile potting soil and clean pots or trays. Try not to sow the seeds too thickly. Remember to label the flats after the seeds go in. So many seedlings look alike that they're easy to mix up.

Tomatoes are what are called "heavy feeders". This means that they use up a lot of the nutrients in the soil where they are planted. Now is a good time to plan ahead for their future quarters. This is where the cow manure and the earthworms come in. So go ahead and fill up the back of your car.

March

Forcing & Pruning

his winter has been so mild that the soil in my garden was never frozen solid. There were a few very cold days when the top layer was frozen, but then along came another thawing rain and the ground was soft again. Now the buds on many of the spring flowering shrubs are swollen early.

When the buds begin to swell, it is a good time to cut some branches to bring in for forcing (bringing into bloom before it's natural time). Forsythia, pussy willow and flowering quince are easy to force into bloom. Lilacs are more difficult to force, but I've noticed that the buds are big very early this year and they might be worth a try.

Branches of fruit trees can be forced into bloom indoors but they can take longer so make sure you have the patience to wait up to a few weeks for flowers before you make these cuts. Magnolia and dogwood have architectural flowering branches that look sensational in an indoor arrangement.

Try to find branches of whatever you are cutting, that are 2 to 3 feet long with lots of buds. Make your cuts with a sharp knife, hand pruners or heavy scissors in an inconspicuous place on the plant where you won't notice the spaces later. Make a one or two inch slit up the bottom of the stem to help the branch absorb water more easily. You can also lightly bash the end of the stem with a hammer but I'd rather not do that (plant abuse).

Immerse the whole branch in a tub of room temperature water for a few hours to soften the buds so they will open easier. This is especially important for the more woody stems. Then place in a tall container of water that is changed often (every few days) to keep clean of bacteria. Mist the buds of the woody plants daily until they open.

apple

Forsythia and pussy willow blossoms will usually open easily, just by being brought inside and put in a vase of water. They will often form roots on the stems and you can plant them outside later in the spring after the last frost.

If you don't have any flowering shrubs or trees to prune for forcing you can ask your nice neighbor if you can cut a few branches. Then you can force a few for the both of you. This is where I could say, "May the force be with you," but I won't.

While you're outside looking for branches for forcing, look around at your shrubs and trees and think about pruning. This is a good time to cut out dead branches and see the true shape of the plant before it starts to leaf out.

Some shrubs flower on the branches that they make this year. This is a good time to trim them to encourage new branches for more flowers. Examples of this are: *buddliea* (the orange-eyed butterfly bush), *hibiscus* and *abelia*.

Wait to prune shrubs such as lilac, mock orange, daphne, rhododendron, viburnum, and hydrangeas because you will miss out on this years bloom if you prune them now. They flower on "old wood" or last year's branches. After they bloom, you can prune to improve the plant shape or size and to promote "new wood".

Fruit growers are pruning now. I saw people pruning in grape orchards this past week. If you have overgrown blueberry bushes, now is a good time to cut out some of the old branches. Try cutting out 1/3 of the old blueberry wood this year and 1/3 next year to encourage new fruiting branches.

If you want to do some tree pruning, the general rule is "if you have to use a ladder, call a professional". Don't prune maples now because the sap will run excessively. Wait until later in the summer or fall to trim maples.

Before you go out with your shiny new pruners or loppers, think about what shape the shrub or tree grows naturally. Heavy pruning at the incorrect time can greatly shorten the life of your plants. Pruning done at the right time can help keep plants healthy and attractive.

A few pruning rules that can apply to all your outdoor plants are: remove dead, dying and diseased branches, cut out suckers (the upright branches that grow out of the tree base), cut out crossing or rubbing branches, thin out to let in air and light, and remove overly long and awkward branches that look out of place.

Pruning is a garden chore that I enjoy.
No kneeling involved.

Passionflowers

Spring is coming early this year. The early crocus and the late crocus are out at the same time. There are red buds already on the swamp maples. The blue primroses are out at the same time as the yellow witch hazel. The progression of spring flowering plants is all jumbled up.

It's been so tempting to remove the mulch on the perennial beds but I think it's too early. March can bite the tender shoots with a sudden freeze.

In my yard, there are hosta beds that are under planted with daffodils. After the hosta foliage dies down in the fall, I cover the beds with oak leaves. Usually this mulch can be removed in the spring when the daffodil foliage starts up and the leaves have time to toughen up before the buds come out. This warm winter has caused the leaves and buds to shoot up together to full height with mulch still around their ankles. It will be more difficult to remove the mulch now without damaging the daffodils.

Every year is different. That's something I like about gardening on Cape Cod. If you are looking for something different to grow in your garden this year, why not try a passion flower?

Passifloraceae is a tropical based genus but there are members of this exotic family that will winter over in our Cape Cod gardens. Once you see a passion flower blossom, you never forget it.

There is a species of passion flower that is native to the United States called Passiflora incarnata with the common name, "May Pop" or "May Apple". The May Pop has incredible, sweetly scented 3 inch flowers with a variety of flower colors on the same vine - whites, pinks and lilacs. It also has edible yellow fruit.

May Pop seeds should be planted indoors now (Feb. - April) and kept in a warm and sunny location until they can be planted outside later in the spring. Seeds are available from catalogues or through the Passiflora Society International if you join. Soak the seeds for a few hours in warm water before planting to increase germination.

Plant outside in May after danger of frost in a sheltered, sunny location with something for them to climb on like a fence or a trellis. The vines can grow up to 20 - 30 feet in one season then die back to the ground in the winter.

It is best to plant this hardy passion flower in an isolated spot away from other flower beds. The vigorous fleshy roots can send up suckers for quite a distance, but they are easy to pull out in places where you don't want them.

If you'd rather not start from seeds, passion flower plants are available from some local nurseries later in the spring. This plant can also be grown from cuttings taken in the summer.

Passiflora caerulea - the blue passion flower is also hardy here when grown in sheltered areas. There are hundreds of different passion flower vines that can be grown here as annuals or inside as container specimens for year round color and fruit. They come in a wide variety of flower size and color. The leaf shapes may vary, but the flower shapes are all basically the same.

In warmer parts of the world there are butterflies that play a major part in the life of passion flowers. Many butterfly species exist only on specific passion flower vines. There have been a lot of studies on the relationship between butterflies and passion flowers.

Ron Boender, the founder of Butterfly World in Florida is also the founder of the Passiflora Society International. In 1989, he started the society with fifteen members. Currently there are hundreds of members from all over the world who exchange seeds, information on various passiflora and biographies of the members. The annual dues of $15. includes an attractive quarterly newsletter filled with passion flower news.

Passiflora Society International
c/o Butterfly World
3600 W. Sample Rd.
Coconut Creek, FL 33073

Indoor Citrus

he days are getting noticeably longer and the gardeners are itchy to get outside and grow things. It's March. Some days the garden is frozen hard as cement, and some days it's a muddy mess. The garden plans for the summer are ready in our heads if not on paper but it's still too early for most of us to put them into action.

If your little green thumb needs a new project, you can try growing plants from that great seed source: the fruit aisle of the grocery store. Try getting your seed from the actual fruit instead of the pretty seed packet.

Now I'm not saying that you'll be able to grow plants that will produce exact copies of the fruit where you got the seed, but you can get beautiful tropical plants for your sunny window sill that will produce fragrant flowers and sometimes fruit.

Every time you spit out seeds from a tangerine or orange, you're getting rid of a possible plant. Kids have heard that if they swallow seeds, plants will grow in their stomachs but this just isn't true.

To grow citrus plants, look for ripe fruit and remove the seeds. Almost any citrus with seeds will do: oranges, grapefruit, lemons, limes, tangerines, etc. To increase the germination rate and speed up the process, place the seeds between layers of damp paper towels, seal in a zip lock bag and put in a warm place such as the top of the refrigerator. Check in a few days, the seed should have a little root poking out. You can skip the paper towel step if you want to and go directly to planting the seed in damp potting soil mixed with sterile sand. To sterilize sand, cover with water and boil for a few minutes. Citrus seeds do not need to be planted deeply, one half inch down is okay.

Glossy green leaves will appear shortly and you can increase the pot size as the plant grows. Grapefruit can quickly grow into a very large plant so you might want to try lemon, lime or tangerine for a smaller plant. Don't be afraid to prune to keep the plant to a manageable size and shape.

Most citrus plants are self-fruitful. This means that the flowers on a plant can pollinate flowers on the same plant. Some other plants, such as apples, need flowers from different plants to complete pollination. You can enjoy the sweet smelling blossoms of the citrus plants; but if you want to see fruit on those little trees, you'll have to pollinate the flowers.

48

When the citrus plant is mature enough to make flowers, you will have to be the one to pollinate them unless you have a house full of bees. Take a clean art type paintbrush and lift some pollen (yellow powdery stuff) and brush it onto the female part of another flower (the short sticky stem protruding from the center of the flower). The resulting fruit will probably be a sour, poor tasting thing but it will be beautiful on a little tree that you grew from seed.

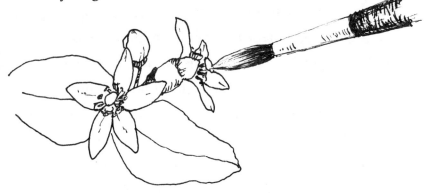

Feed the citrus tree with liquid fertilizer regularly and let it dry out between watering. Put it outside for the summer and water frequently. To discourage the major pests, which are whitefly and mealybug, mist the leaves often with water and inspect the undersides of the leaves for any signs of insects.

Pineapples can also be grown from fruit found at the grocery store. Select a pineapple with a healthy looking, leafy top. This will grow to be the new plant. It is in the Bromeliad family and can do very well as a house plant.

Cut off the pineapple top and lay it on it's side to dry for a few days. When the exposed tissue has hardened and dried, brush on a small amount of rooting hormone and put in a pot filled with potting mix and sand (same mix as for citrus). Water from above letting the water sit in the leaves for a few hours before it evaporates or is absorbed. The leaves will grow and new ones will form making a very attractive plant.

To trigger fruit to form on a mature plant, place a freshly peeled banana skin on the soil next to the pineapple foliage and cover the whole thing with clear plastic. Move out of direct sun. The ethylene gas given off from the banana peel encourages the pineapple to make fruit. In a few weeks, the plant should send up a stalk with a new small pineapple. Remove the plastic. The pineapple will need to be staked because it can get quite top heavy.

Some other grocery store fruit to try growing on from the seeds are kiwi, avocado, star fruit and papaya.

Soil

Put a five dollar plant in a ten dollar hole. This is not an exact dollar figure, but you get the picture. Without healthy soil, you won't have healthy plants. This goes for indoor as well as outdoor gardening.

Plants get most of what they need to grow from the soil. Soil provides the base for support, the habitat for roots and the access for water and nutrients that all plants need. Good soil management maintains a balance of minerals, organic matter, air and water that can be readily used by all plants from grass to trees.

On Cape Cod, for the most part, we have sandy soil. There are veins of clay that run here and there, you certainly know it if you have clay in your yard, and there are places from Eastham to Ptown that have sandy sand rather than sandy soil. Water drains quickly through sandy soil. Dissolved nutrients tend to drain out with the water leaving our soil relatively infertile. But no matter what texture your soil is, it can be improved to increase the yield from any type of garden.

Adding organic matter is probably the most important thing you can do to improve your soil. Organic matter is the decayed remains of plants, animals and soil organisms. This is nature's recycling program.

Organic matter added to soil improves the structure for both sand and clay. It makes a texture that is easier for roots as well as earthworms to move through. It improves the fertility, providing nutrients that plants need for growth and encourages a healthy population of microorganisms that help break down decaying matter.

Organic amendments should be tilled into the soil before spring planting and again after harvesting. It can be applied as a mulch during the growing season. If you use a roto-tiller to mix in amendments, be careful not to over do it and grind your soil into powder. This ground up soil will turn into cement after the first rain. When you can't add organic matter directly into the soil, such as around trees and shrubs, it can be added as a surface layer a few inches thick to provide a slow-release source of nutrients.

You can buy bags of organic matter such as peat moss and cow manure at the garden centers or you can make your own compost, a free source for balanced nutrients. There are many ways to make compost from the easiest: make a pile of garden and kitchen waste and leave it until it breaks down into humus, to the expensive and complicated: buy special bins with turning mechanisms. But whatever method of composting you decide to use, the end product has great benefits for the garden. The libraries and county extension office have a lot of material about compost if you want to learn more.

After you determine your soil type (sandy, clay, loam) you might want to have a sample tested for pH. The correct soil pH makes the nutrients more easily available for intake through the plant roots. PH is a measure of how acid or alkaline a liquid is. For a pH soil test, a small amount (few teaspoons) of your soil is mixed with distilled water then measured with a pH meter. The pH scale goes from 1 through 14, with 1 being the most acid, 14 being the most alkaline, and 7 being neutral. Most plants grow best when the soil pH is around 6.5 to 7. This is the range where elements in the soil will dissolve in water and be able to be taken up by the roots.

Not all plants need the same pH. For example, blueberries and rhododendrons need a lower pH - 4.5 to 5.5. Cabbages and other cole crops do better with a higher pH of 7.2. Some plants are so pH specific that they will not grow unless the soil is adjusted to fit their needs. If the pH is too high or too low, you can add ingredients to make your soil recipe come out just right.

You can have your soil tested at the Extension Service office in Barnstable for $2.00. Or you can bring a soil sample to any of the many soil test clinics this spring.

April

Strawberries

It is a well known fact that two of the most important words in the English language are *strawberry* and *shortcake*. Strawberries can be grown in every Cape Cod garden. The shortcake . . . well you have to grow that in your kitchen.

Strawberries have been cultivated in gardens for hundreds of years. Their tiny wild cousins are found in many parts of the world from planting zones 3 through 10. Bare root strawberry plants are available now at local nurseries and this is a good time for planting. There are many varieties available that are suitable for Cape Cod. They are easy to grow and require little space. You can even grow strawberries in containers.

When choosing strawberry plants, you will find four groups: the June bearing, the ever bearing, the day neutrals and the alpines. The term, June bearing doesn't necessarily mean that they only fruit in June; it refers to plants that only fruit once a year. This group is further divided into *early, mid, and late* varieties with a week or more between ripening time for each division.

Alpines are the tiny fruited plants that have strong strawberry flavor. These plants have other garden uses in addition to their value for fruit. They can be used for groundcover or as an attractive edging plant. Some alpines have white fruit and there are varieties with pretty variegated leaves.

For the longest season of strawberries, choose plants from more than one group. Plants from the ever bearing, June bearing and day neutral types look the same at purchase but have different cultural practices for the best fruit. Twenty five plants will make enough fruit for a family of four including storage.

Locate your strawberry patch in a sunny location. Strawberries will grow in almost any soil type with sandy loam as a preferred site. Add some aged cow or horse manure, lime if the pH is too low, and some 10 - 10 - 10 fertilizer to the soil the FIRST year. After the first year, do not apply fertilizer in the spring because too much nitrogen results in large, bland, soft berries and excessive vegetative growth.

If your new strawberry patch is not prepared yet, and you want to buy plants now, soak the roots of the new plants, then heel in (plant temporarily) into a moist shady spot until they can be planted permanently. Don't worry about the cold.

It is important to plant new strawberries at the correct depth. There is a collar between the fibrous roots and where the leaves come out. The soil surface should be right in the middle of this collar.

There are several systems for planting strawberries and each one requires some maintenance except for the alpines which you can just plant and stand back. The most common is the matted row system where plants are set 12 to 24 inches apart in rows that are 2 to 3 feet apart. There are other methods of planting such as single and double hedgerows and hill systems. Different methods use the runners that the plants send out.

Mulch the strawberry plants with clean straw, not hay, (they're straw-berries not hay-berries) to keep down weeds and prevent wet soil from touching the fruit. Also use straw to cover the plants over the winter after cutting off the leaves.

Now this is the most difficult part of raising strawberries: for June bearing as well as all ever bearing plants, it is important to remove the first blossoms of the first year. Yes, this means that there will be no fruit on the June bearers this year and only late fruit on the ever bearers. Plants that are allowed to fruit on the first year will be weaker and less fruitful in successive seasons. Remove any plants that do not produce flowers the first season. If the rows look too sparse the first year, interplant with fast growing lettuce or radishes. Control weeds by pulling them when they are small. Eradicate all garden weeds before they compete for space, nutrients, water and your patience.

Soaker hoses are a great method of irrigation for strawberries because the soil can be kept moist without splashing the fruit and leaves which encourages fungal diseases. Strawberries need about one inch of water a week in the summer.

Strawberry plants start to send out runners in July until frost. Most of these should be removed. If the plants become too crowded, they will produce smaller and smaller fruit. You can put some of the runners into 4" pots filled with potting soil while they are still attached to the mother plant. After about six weeks, the well-rooted runners can be cut off and the potted plants given to friends.

Harvest strawberries (one for the basket, two for me) when they are fully colored and sweet. The taste test for ripeness is most effective. Leave the stems on for better storage. There are lots of recipes for this well loved fruit as well as just freezing for winter use. And we all know that when the strawberries are ripe, shortcake season is not far behind.

Peas

As soon as there is even a hint of spring in the air, something deep in my gardening soul screams, "MUST PLANT PEAS!" This usually starts sometime in January, but I resist planting peas until the time when the crocus is fully up in March or the beginning of April.

Garden peas are a terrific plant to get children or beginners interested in gardening. They are very easy to grow. The seeds go directly into the ground and germinate quickly. Harvesting time is early, sometimes even before other vegetables go in the garden. Peas can be eaten right from the vine!

Peas are a cool weather crop. If you wait until Memorial Day to plant peas with your other vegetables, they won't do as well as if they were planted now. Cape Cod summers are usually too hot for peas planted late.

There are many varieties of peas to choose from. Read the packages in the stores or seed catalogs to see if the plants will be of dwarf habit (bush type), or tall habit.

Peas are also called the shelling type - where the pods are full of plump peas in a tougher outer shell, snap peas - full size peas with a softer, edible shell, and snowpeas or sugar peas which are grown for the shells and should be harvested while still flat before the peas develop.

In the garden, choose a site for peas that is in full sun with good air circulation. Peas will tolerate partial shade in the warmer months but will need full sun in the spring. Although peas are tough and disease resistant, the leaves are sometimes afflicted with powdery mildew when there is not enough air circulation around the plants.

Any fertile garden soil with a pH of 6.0 to 6.8 is good for peas. They tolerate a wide range of soil types but will do best when the soil is loose and mixed with organic matter. Fertilizer is usually not necessary.

For tall growing peas, plant in single rows with the trellis supports in place at time of planting. The fast growing vines do better when they can grow up a supporting structure. Peas attach themselves to supports with curling tendrils. There are lots of ways to brace up tall habit peas, just have the trellis tall enough to encourage full growth, the seed package should say the height.

Well branched yard brush can be used for trellis material. Make sure it is firmly affixed to the ground so it won't blow away and take your peas with it. Some people use string trellis. Chicken wire or other garden fencing between posts is a reusable trellis. Tall garden stakes can be formed into a teepee and covered with wire or string for use in a limited space.

Dwarf varieties also benefit from supports to keep the vines off the ground. The shorter growing peas can also be grown in containers on a sunny deck or patio. Attach a trellis to a large pot at planting time and use potting soil instead of garden soil because frequent watering will pack down garden soil and suffocate the plant.

In the garden, trellised peas make a great wind block for other vegetables such as tomatoes and eggplant. Lettuce and spinach will grow better when grown in the shade of the pea plants. Carrots, radishes, turnips and parsnips are good neighbors for peas. Don't grow peas next to onions or garlic. Underplant peas with caraway plants because they mature slowly and fill in when the peas die off. The pretty caraway plant has flowers that resemble queen-anne's-lace, and nutty seeds with a licorice-like taste.

Garden peas are a good crop for anyone with a garden - even if you don't like the taste of peas.

All plants take some nutrients from the soil as they grow, but some, including peas, return more than they consume. Nitrogen fixing bacteria colonizes along the roots of peas (and other legumes) and converts nitrogen in the air into nitrogen compounds that plants can use. The peas don't use all of the nitrogen that is produced. When the nodule bearing roots die off and decompose, they leave nitrogen available for new plants. This is why you shouldn't pull up and discard the peas when then are finished. Turn the foliage and the roots back into the soil.

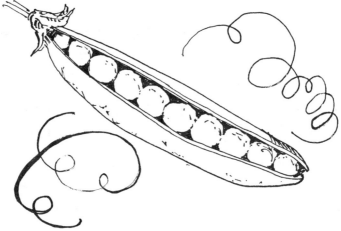

Next year, put in pumpkins, watermelons or corn where the peas are now to benefit from the improved soil. Unlike tomatoes or many other vegetables, peas can be grown in the same place for years. But the peas won't grow until you heed the primal spring voice and get out there to plant them.

Hummingbirds

This year when you're choosing new flowers for the garden, remember to grow something for the hummingbirds. Hummingbirds feed on copious quantities of nectar that you can help to provide with flowers as well as hummingbird feeders.

Although their numbers are declining in nature, there are still lots of hummingbirds that return to Cape Cod each spring from their winter migration to Florida and Central America. You can attract and keep the little hovering jewels by planting nectar rich perennials and annuals in your garden and hanging a nectar feeder outside. If you don't like the red plastic hummingbird feeders, there are some nice ones being sold at the local pottery shops.

Hummingbirds are attracted to the color red but they will also visit many different colored flowers all summer. Once when my daughter was three or four, she was wearing a white shirt with a little red sailboat embroidered on the sleeve. A hummingbird followed her around the yard, hovering a few inches away from the red boat.

Although there are many kinds of humming-birds, the ruby-throated hummingbird is the only species to visit here. With their tiny body and high level of activity, they have the highest metabolic rate of any animal, including chipmunks and cub scouts.

Hummingbirds return to the same nesting area each year so if you can attract some to your garden, you might be lucky enough to keep them coming back. The female builds a tiny cup shaped nest from plant fibers bound with spider silk. She covers and camouflages the nest with moss and lichen. You can sometimes spot the tiny nests on down-sloping evergreen branches.

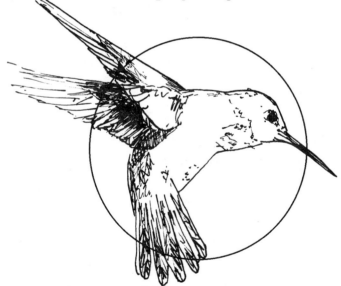

Although my personal preference is for flowers in the blues and purples, a little bit of red makes a great accent to sharpen color in any garden. Tubular shaped red flowers are particularly attractive to hummingbirds.

Annual flowers that are good to entice the hummingbird to stay are nasturtiums, morning glories, snapdragons, red impatiens and cosmos. Fuchsias and petunias in hanging baskets are hummingbird magnets. Lobelia cardinalis and pineapple sage have tall stems with bright red flowers to bring the hummers in.

Members of the campsis family (trumpet vine or trumpet creeper) have tubular flowers in reds, oranges and yellows the come out in August and last for a long time. This vine can take a few years to get established but once it gets going it is very vigorous. So plant it on a sturdy support where it will have room to spread. Honeysuckle vines also have good tubular flowers for hummingbirds.

There are some flowers that hummingbirds love that are considered invasive for the garden bed. In other words, they can take over if you let them get ahead of you. These include: bee balm *monarda* , loosestrife *lythrum,* lupine, foxglove, Joe Pye weed and rose campion.   I'm not saying don't plant these, just be cautious where they go in the garden.

Most of the daisy shaped flowers are rich in nectar and attractive to butterflies as well as hummingbirds.

red penstemon

Summer phlox also has a lot of sweet nectar; the similarly shaped Maltese cross *lychnis* makes a small red feature in a perennial bed. Day lilies, hollyhocks, columbines and iris are popular nectar sites. Delphiniums and their easier to grow cousins the larkspurs have blue flowers with iridescent qualities that attract hummingbirds.

Hummingbirds supplement their sweet diet with spiders and small insects. With wings that beat 55 to 75 times per second, hummingbirds need lots of food for energy. Keep a look out for the tiny iridescent green hummingbird. The male has a glowing red throat and the female has a less noticeable white throat. They should be arriving in our gardens soon.

Yellow

Yellow is the color that is taking center stage now in the spring garden. Daffodil, forsythia, dreaded dandelion, yellow primrose. The grass is greening up and already needs to be trimmed in places. Green is a good background for yellow flowers.

There are many yellow flowering and yellow foliage plants to choose from to brighten up any garden space. Pretty soon the brilliant yellow colored basket of gold *aurinia saxitilis* will be cascading over garden walls. The sunny or pale yellow broom *cytisus* shrubs will soon have their masses of pea like flowers swaying in the late spring breezes of Cape Cod. The broom shrubs thrive here in our sandy soil. They should be trimmed back right after flowering time to encourage a more manageable size. When left without trimming, the broom becomes woody and leggy and not as full flowering. Replace every five years or so with a new broom shrub. There are also more colors of broom to choose from at the nurseries but the focus today is on yellow.

Some yellow flowering perennials that have a long season of bloom and not much need for fussing include: various yarrows, *achillea* - 'coronation gold', 'moonbeam', 'moonshine', members of the *coreopsis* family 'threadleaf', 'lanceleaf', 'tickseed', the small yellow daylily, 'Stella de Oro', garden goldenrod, verbascums, sundrops *oenothera*, yellow loosestrife (beautiful but invasive, be careful where this goes), sneezeweeds *heleniums*, and some of the new sunflowers like 'Teddybear'. The globeflower, *trollius* has outstanding yellow blossoms on 2' tall stems. They look like giant buttercups.

Yellow flowering perennials that do well in shady areas are leopard's bane *doronicum cordatum*, golden star *chrysogonum virginanum*, and yellow bells, also called *kirengeshoma palmata*.

There is an ornamental grass called zebra grass *miscanthus sinensis* 'Zebrinus' that grows 6 to 8 feet tall. It has medium green leaves with horizontal yellow stripes going across the leaves. It is a very interesting plant that grows well here in a sunny spot. It does not like to dry out, however, and does better with a fertile soil. Place it where it will have room to make a big clump. It is generally not a good idea to put most of the ornamental grasses in the perennial beds because they will get too big and should be divided every few years.

My friend, Roberta, says that she is going to need a chainsaw to divide her three year old miscanthus. It's way past the kitchen knife dividing stage. But zebra grass is still worth the trouble. Those yellow horizontal stripes are unusual.

Potentilla is a small shrub that has yellow (and other colored) flowers that last for a long season. The small rounded shrub with the little grey-green leaves can be entirely covered with yellow blossoms. It is a nice addition as an edging plant but it should never dry out.

Yellow or golden marguerites and marigolds are annuals that are staples in many Cape Cod gardens. There are clear yellow dahlias and lantanas for long summer blooms.

For the winter garden there is a golden twig dogwood, sometimes called yellow-stem dogwood. The branches on this shrub are bright yellow all winter after the leaves have fallen off in the fall. It truly stands out in the winter landscape.

The branches of the dogwood shrubs should be cut back to the ground in late winter to encourage new growth. The branches will turn grey with age, it is the new sprout that is yellow for a year.

There is a native American plant called yellowroot. It is in the buttercup family. When broken, both the stem and roots are an intense yellow. There are yellow lady slippers. The little butter-and-eggs that grow wild all over Cape look like miniature yellow snapdragons. The fragrant yellow evening primrose will appear later in the summer.

The golden-chain tree, *laburnum* has golden wisteria-like blossoms in June that are 18 to 24" long. There is also a golden-rain tree, *koelreuteria* that has similar blossoms later in the summer. The yellowwood tree, *cladrastis lutea* has yellow blossoms in the fall.

There are yellow flowers from a to z (azalea to zinnia). I almost forgot rudbeckia - the queen of the late summer. Must stop. Yellow yucca. Yellow tulips. Yellow rose. Yellow crocus. Yellow iris. Help! Yellow Japanese maple. Yellow hosta. Yellow lily . . .

May

Ode To The Earthworm

After all the rain that we've been having, have you noticed the little mounds of structured mud all over the lawn and in the garden? These are the *casts* or *castings* from the earthworms that live in our soil. The castings are full of useful nutrients, but if you find them too unsightly on the lawn, they can be raked over.

Earthworms are beneficial to gardeners as well as being an important link in the food chain. Ask any robin! As they tunnel and feed, earthworms make our soil more productive by improving the structure and fertility. They eat soil for the organic matter that it contains.

Aristotle called earthworms the "intestines of the earth" and Darwin said they were the "earth's plow". Exulted by poets and fishermen as well as the Cape Cod gardener, the earthworm has a place in the hearts of all but the most squeamish.

It's great to find lots of earthworms when you're turning over the soil in your garden. This is an indication of healthy soil with a neutral pH. Earthworms thrive in moist, well aerated soil that is full of organic matter.

For that matter so do most of our garden plants. The earthworms live on the decaying plant matter in the soil and in turn produce valuable castings which are loaded with the nitrogen, phosphorus, potassium, and micro-nutrients that the plants need.

Earthworm activity lightens the soil and makes it pervious to air and water. They also mix the soil, carry organic matter deep below the surface and bring the subsoil up. Their burrows can be six feet long. When the weather is too hot, too cold or too dry, the earthworms go deep into the soil.

Unfortunately just adding a handful of earthworms to poor soil will probably not do much to improve it. Don't add them to a pile of sand or clay and expect to get rich loam. This must be done together with adding organic matter such as compost, peat, manure and/or ground up decaying plant material.

If you add it, they will come.

Contrary to cartoon versions of earthworms, such as Larson's 'Far Side' with worms sitting on sofas, reading newspapers, earthworms do not have eyes. They are sensitive to light, however, particularly at their front end. If you go out tonight and shine a flashlight onto a nightcrawler, it will immediately try to shrink back into its burrow.

Earthworms do not have teeth either. Their mouth and pharynx are highly muscular for grinding food. The mouth is hidden in the first (anterior) segment of the earthworm. It is opened and closed when the worm expands and contracts as it moves along in search of suitable particles to ingest.

There is a popular myth that earthworms will make two new earthworms when they are cut in half. I hate to be a debunker, but this just isn't true. The anterior section can regenerate a new tail, but the tail can't grow a new front end. Occasionally, you will find a worm with two tails. This happens when there is an injury and a new tail is grown next to the old one.

In 1881, Darwin estimated that earthworms deposited from eight to eighteen tons of nutrient rich castings per acre in pasture land. This has been shown to be a conservative estimate with today's research.

In my vegetable garden, I counted 57 earthworms in a square foot, digging down six or seven inches. There are 43,560 square feet in an acre so this would average 2,482,920 earthworms per acre here if there are as many in the grass as in the gardens. (garden math and science)

Chemical fertilizers and pesticides, with their caustic salts, reduce the earthworm and microbial populations in our soil. Consequently, there is less organic matter available for the plants when these are applied.

While earthworms are encouraged in the garden, they should not be put in with container grown plants. Their busy activity quickly ruins the balance in a potted plant. In no time, the pot is filled with worms and there is havoc among the roots. If you see castings on top of the soil of indoor or outdoor potted plants, it is time to repot and evict the earthworms. Send them off to the garden where they will be welcomed.

Lady's Mantle

Lady's Mantle *Alchemilla* is an easy to grow plant that can find a home in almost any kind of garden. It has unusual, attractive yellow-green or grey-green scalloped leaves that appear to have been pleated as they open. If you use your imagination, they look like the folds in a medieval cloak - hence the common name Lady's Mantle.

The name *Alchemilla* is latinized from the Arabic name for the plant where it was originally grown in Eastern Europe. Our garden variety of Alchemilla has been developed from the plants that grew wild in Europe. But they can also still be found growing in mountainous regions of South America, Africa and India.

In cultivation for hundreds of years, many people grow this plant just for the interesting leaves and cut off the flowers as they appear in July. The long lasting, airy, yellow-green flowers stand up to ten inches above the eight to ten inch high foliage and sway in the summer breezes of Cape Cod. The flowers are good for use by arrangers because they can be a subtle space filler.

Sprays of the light green Alchemilla flowers go well with bouquets of roses which are sometimes difficult to mix with other flowers in arrangements. Alchemilla flowers also dry easily and keep their color for a long time.

Chartreuse is a "hot" color in the landscape garden now; especially when mixed with the burgundy colored foliage plants such as the smoke bush *cotinus* , the red 'crimson queen' barberry, or the 'palace purple' heuchera. The Alchemilla is a good plant to spill over the perimeter of a garden walkway, over a wall, along the edge of a water garden or in a rockery.

Virtually foolproof when grown from seed, division, or nursery bought plants, the Alchemilla is  well behaved in the garden. The plant will increase in size from year to year but it will not spread out and take over. Divide in the spring or fall to move to other places in the garden or a friend's garden. You will probably find small Alchemilla plants that have self-seeded, but they pull out easily if they appear in an inconvenient spot.

Lady's Mantle is a herbaceous perennial which means that it dies back to the ground in the winter and comes back in the spring. It is easily grown in full sun or partial shade. I have found that if it is planted in a hot, sunny place, it needs more water and sometimes will get a little leggy by August. You can cut it back and get new fresh foliage in the same season.

Alchemilla can be combined with other plants for window boxes and patio containers. It looks especially nice next to blue campanulas, although I admit that I like anything next to blue campanulas. Also a member of the rose family, Alchemilla does well when grown at the feet of roses. The round leaves of the Lady's Mantle are a nice contrast against the long narrow foliage of iris. Variety of leaf shape in the perennial bed makes for a longer season of interest because many flowers only last for a short time.

There are varieties of Alchemilla that come with red leaves and stems or small leafed versions but these plants are not widely available. The Alchemilla that is usually sold here is the *Alchemilla vulgaris* , also called Alchemilla mollis.

Lady's Mantle has no serious disease or insect problems. It even appears to be deer resistant, but a hungry deer will eat just about anything. It is considered a herb although it is not grown as an edible plant.

The leaves of the Alchemilla hold drops of dew with reflecting air bubbles that shine like jewels for hours in the morning garden. Medieval alchemists made up aphrodisiacs from the drops collected from the leaves of the Alchemilla. Maybe modern day alchemists do too.

Clematis

There is a cherry tree raining (snowing) down white petals from spent blossoms outside the window of the room where I write. It is difficult to concentrate. The month of May is just about perfect to this gardener's way of thinking.

At the garden center a few days ago, I saw a clematis vine that I could not resist. It is a large flowering double purple one. Sooner or later I'll figure out where to plant it.

The clematis vine is a beautiful and popular ornament for our gardens. Mature plants can provide us with clouds of flowers and masses of foliage that clamber up and over supports.

Clematis is a member of the buttercup family *Ranunculaceae*. Its name comes from a Greek name for a climbing plant. In the wild, it is found in many places of the northern hemisphere from the warm regions of the Mediterranean to the mountains of China. There are wild clematis in Texas, Nepal, France and Korea.

There are hundreds of named varieties of clematis that are in cultivation today. They are still being hybridized to increase the flower size, colors and hardiness. Most clematis vines are deciduous (their leaves fall off in winter), but there are some evergreen ones. Clematis is known as a late spring/early summer bloomer, but there are fall blooming clematis, and some that have two flowering times a year.

The flowers come in all colors and can be up to nine inches across. The large flowers have no true petals. The colored *petals* are really sepals. After the sepals fall off, many of the clematis have interesting seed pods that persist on the vine until frost. The seed pods are also good for flower arrangements. The blossoms do not last very well as cut flowers.

Clematis are available now at most of the local garden centers and through mail order. This is the best time of year for planting. Some of the large flowering varieties take a few years to reach their maximum flower size but they start to produce blooms at an early age.

They are usually divided up into the large flowering and the species groups. The flowers are smaller in the species group but they make up for it with better vigor and garden performance. The species group usually has flowers with four *petals* and the large flowering group can have dramatic blossoms with many *petals* .

Soil and site preparation are important for success with clematis. They like their head in the sun and their feet in the shade. For the greatest size and number of blossoms, choose a location out of the harshest wind with an East or West facing wall or structure for them to climb. North facing clematis will not produce as many blossoms, and South facing walls may be too hot and dry with Cape Cod summers. South facers will be okay if the feet or bottoms of the vines are hidden by low shrubs or perennials that will not compete for nutrients.

When planting, amend the soil with a lot of cow manure and compost to create a rich well-drained, loose mix. Dig deeply even though the plant will probably be small at purchase time. Clematis prefers a "sweet" pH, so sprinkle the soil (like you were shaking some pepper) with powdered lime around the base of the vine. Top-dress with well-rotted manure, lime and leaf compost each spring.

Clematis is a wonderful companion plant for climbing roses or wisteria. They have similar soil requirements and enhance each other's blossoms. They can be grown on a wall, trellis, arch, pergola, up a tree or through another climber.

On Martha's Vineyard last summer, I saw a rustic, covered bench made from gnarley old locust branches. There were many kinds of clematis vines growing up and over the branches. Very inviting.

There are a few problems with clematis vines. They have a tendency to become bare at the base of the plant. This can be remedied by companion planting. Different clematis plants need different kinds of annual pruning and it can be confusing to remember which one needs which. You can buy a clematis growing guide or keep a catalog such as "Wayside" handy for pruning and growing tips. Then there is the biggest problem with clematis, - how to pronounce the word *clematis*. I looked it up in many sources, the correct way to say it is, "klem - a - tis" with the accent on the first syllabul.

Planting Time

Ready! Set! Go! Time for planting! No more frost, fingers crossed, another trowel lost, forget about the cost!

Is the soil ready? If not, keep those little plants in their pots and seeds in the packets for a bit longer and work on the soil. After a few too many trips to the garden center for soil amendments, promise to start making compost for next year's soil.

Two styles of compost bins are available through the Barnstable County Cooperative Extension. They are about $20. each. These are the same heavy duty bins that sold in national catalogs for a much higher price. Some of the Cape Cod towns still have compost bins for sale if you don't want to drive to the Extension office in Barnstable. Check with your town hall for availability.

I use the compost bin for the household garbage, mixing with leaves or straw to keep down odor. These bins have locking lids to keep raccoons, crows and other garden pests from spreading garbage out all over the yard.

This breaks down quickly and can then be combined with leaf compost for the garden.

As soon as the soil is prepared and not too wet, it's time to plant. When it crumbles like a piece of chocolate cake, the soil is ready. Here are a few tips for planting tomatoes. When you dig a hole to put in the tomato plant, mix in a cup of powdered lime, a cup of 10-10-10 fertilizer, and a cup of epsom salts with the soil in the hole. Make sure the soil is nice and loose all around the new plant for the roots to be able to move.

Tomato support systems should be installed at the time of planting. The roots are shallow and delicate; they can be damaged if you wait until the plants are bigger. Tomato support is not a 12 - Step program, it's the different methods of holding the tomato plants up off the ground. Left to their own habit, tomatoes will sprawl along the ground. Propped up, tomatoes produce earlier fruit and give ground pests and soil borne diseases less access.

Staking is simple and inexpensive but it involves a lot of labor throughout the summer. This method requires pruning and tying. Along about mid-summer, we can get some wicked winds on Cape Cod that can snap even heavy wooden stakes that have tomato plants attached. (The voice of disasters remembered.)

Tall heavy wire or wood caging that is firmly anchored is a reliable support for tomatoes. Those three or four foot tall tomato cages that you can buy are really not adequate for most tomato plants unless they are short, determinate plants or grown in containers.

Trellising with wood, wire or strong string is also a good method of support. Weave the young vines up through the grids each week as they grow, removing the suckers that grow out of the leaf axils. This is also more laborious than the cage method, but it looks darn nice in the vegetable garden.

Try not to grow your tomatoes in the same spot year after year, especially if there has been any evidence of disease. This includes leaf spots, leaf yellowing or blackening, fruit rot or drop. These are soil borne diseases that persist for years.

Remember to harden off tomatoes (and all other young plants) before they go into the garden. Some plants that you get at the garden center or the plant sale come directly from the warm, protective greenhouse. Set these tender plants outside in a sheltered place out of the wind and direct sun for a few days before planting. Bring them in at night or cover them up.

Wait until the soil has thoroughly warmed up before mulching. Tomatoes are tropical plants and they don't like to be cold. Mulch discourages weeds and slows down moisture loss. Try not to use fresh woodchips for mulch. It robs the plants of nitrogen and they will turn yellow or worse.

The best time to fertilize tomatoes is a few weeks after planting, or when the first blossoms appear. Tomatoes are heavy feeders, meaning that they use up a lot of nutrients in the soil to make those big, juicy, can't wait for the first ones, tomatoes.

And one more thing, how about trying a new kind of tomato that you never grew before along next to your old favorites. Happy planting!

June

Lady slippers

If you take a walk in the wilder parts of Cape Cod, not Commercial Street on Saturday night, but out into the pine forests, you might be able to see some pink lady slippers blooming now. I saw a few along the side of a bike trail last week and more inside a certain park. There is something about lady slippers that makes the observer want to keep their location hidden.

The pink lady slipper that grows here on Cape Cod has other common names like - moccasin flower, nerve root, American valprian, and Noah's ark. The botanic name *Cypripedium acaule* comes from the Greek words for "Venus or Aphrodite's shoe" It is in the orchid family.

There are eleven species of cypripedium found in North America. One is the Minnesota state flower. In Massachusetts, there are yellow, pink and white, and pink lady slippers. The pink lady slippers are the ones most likely to be found on Cape Cod.

Each lady slipper bloom seems like such a rarity even when you come upon a group of them.

I have seen white ones in Canada but only pink lady slippers around here. The flower of a lady slipper is like an inflated pink balloon floating above two heavily veined green leaves on the pine forest floor. In an old wildflower book from 1893 called, *How to Know the Wildflowers,* lady slippers were described as having "a fondness for decaying wood, often seen perched like birds along a crumbling log."

Most people know what a pink lady slipper flower looks like. It's exotic form is not easily forgotten. The pink flower stands 6 to 18 inches above the basal leaves. Upon close inspection, you'll see that the flower has tiny red or dark pink veins along the flower sac. These veins point the way for bees to find the nectar and pollen hidden inside the flower.

Lady slippers should never be collected from the wild with the possible exception of saving them from a bulldozer. Beside the fact that it is illegal to remove plants from public or private lands, lady slippers need a very specific environment to survive. Transplants may live for a year or two, but then they will probably die or disappear because of some imperfection in their surroundings. Nursery bought lady slippers do not seem to have a better success rate for garden survival.

Lady slippers will only survive in the micro climate of where they exist in the wild. They are completely dependent on the fungi that live in the natural setting of leaf mold and decaying pine needles on an acidic soil in open shade. These conditions are very difficult to replicate in a garden setting.

Most plant seeds contain food for the young plant as it develops but the lady slipper does not. The fungus, found in the forest floor where the lady slippers grow, attack and digest the outer cells of the lady slipper seeds. Then the inner cells of the minute seeds absorb nutrients from the fungus and then germinate. The young lady slipper corm continues to take its minerals and other nutrients from the fungus.

It takes years for a lady slipper to become mature enough to flower. You'll see many lady slipper leaves and few with flower stems. The average life span of the lady slipper is 20 years and some live much longer.

Douglas Gill, of the University of Maryland, spent sixteen years studying 3,000 pink lady slippers in a national forest. He found that only one third of the plants flowered at that time. Of the 1,000 that flowered, only 23 were successfully pollinated and made seed. It seems like a flower with such a small rate of pollination would die out, but one flower can produce 60,000 seeds.

Lady slippers are very fragrant with a heavy, honey scent if you can get down on your knees to smell them. Bees are attracted from far away to the scent. Lady slippers need bees for cross-pollination to make seed. The bees crawl inside the "slipper" to get at the sweet nectar and the pick up the sticky pollen. If the bee flies to another lady slipper, some of the pollen might stick to the stigma as the bee crawls inside for more nectar. (Birds and bees lesson.)

The fibrous roots of the lady slipper have been used medicinally as a nerve tonic. But use caution if you're going to touch a lady slipper plant. The tiny hairs on the leaves and stems can give you a poison ivy - like rash.

Look for the pink lady slipper flowers in May and June in the pine forests of the parks and wild lands. For me, of all the wild flowers, it seems most to be touched with the spirit of the deep woods.

Animal Pests

The sweet little brown rabbit that scampers across meadows can quickly become a varmint when it gets near your garden. When the deer eats your new hosta garden down to the ground, it transforms into a big brown rat. Then there's the woodchuck - the intrepid devil who lives to eat your tender plants. And let's not forget the cutest of the garden scoundrels, our Cape Cod chipmunk.

There is a commercial industry dedicated to the control of animal and insect pests, but there are some things you can do on your own to limit the damage done by the "garden thugs". Animal repellents and scare tactics, such as plastic owls and snakes, are not dependable control methods to keep your flowers and vegetables safe.

Live traps seem like an effective way of getting rid of animal pests, but it is illegal to take wild animals away anyplace off your property. What are you going to do? Bring them over to the other corner of your yard and set them free? Even if you do trap or get rid of an offending animal, another one will soon show up to take its place.

So the effective options left are constructing barriers such as fences, netting, coverings, or planting things that the animals won't eat. A hungry deer will eat just about anything including plants that are listed as poisonous. I've seen deer eat poisonous rhododendron buds and chew on new shoots of monkshood which is definitely poisonous.

Preventive planting to deter deer from coming to the garden is usually futile. The scented soap bags and other things marketed as deer repellents don't always work. Did you know that you can buy containers of fox or coyote urine to put on sponges stuck in the garden to scare animal pests away. This is a ten dollar a pint, unreliable (and stinky) deer deterrent.

Electric, tall wire, or net fencing are the only relatively dependable deer prevention. I say "relatively" because deer can leap over six foot tall fencing easily. They usually won't jump over a fence unless they have a lot of landing room on the other side. Fencing and its installation can be expensive. There is tall, plastic netting available that blends into the landscape better and is less expensive than wire, but it will not hold up as long and will have to be replaced after a few seasons.

Fencing is also the best deterrent against rabbits and woodchucks. Woodchucks have been known to climb over and dig under fences. They can be a ten pound eating machine in the garden if they are allowed entrance. If you can find and block the burrows where they live, woodchucks will sometimes move to another area which is hopefully far away from your garden. Woodchucks can be fierce fighters and it's better to avoid close contact with them.

Rabbits and woodchucks are a little more fussy about what they eat than deer. They will avoid poisonous plants. Here are a few plants for the flower beds that the cute little vermin will usually leave alone: delphinium and larkspur, iris, impatiens, lily of the valley, lupine, foxglove, yarrow, wormwood, asters, lamb's  ears, sedum, hydrangeas, four o'clocks, columbine and lavender.

My neighbor and I keep our newly planted dahlias covered with crates or wire baskets until the plants are fairly big because the woodchucks and rabbits love to eat the young shoots. They leave the large dahlias alone (and go for other more tender garden plants).

Hungry cats might keep chipmunks out of the garden. Cats can also be destructive in a garden. Some cats think raised beds are large sized litter boxes. Catnip plants can be flattened by all the cats in the neighborhood. Sturdy wire fencing is all that will keep the chipmunks out of the strawberry beds. I tried plastic netting held down with bricks, but the chipmunks got under and took little bites out of lots of strawberries.

So that's what you get when you live in the country and you want to have a garden. Birds and bugs and wild animals are there to compete with you for the bounty. You have to decide how much damage you're willing to put up with and how much time and money you're willing to spend on control. We figure that home grown tomatoes cost about twenty dollars apiece.

Garden Blues

My imaginary flower garden is filled with blue flowers. Tall blue flowers, short blue flowers. Vines with blue flowers. Trees and shrubs with blue flowers. Maybe a couple of bluebirds flying around.

In real life, a garden made up of all blue flowers is visually boring. A blue garden needs other contrasting colors to add dimension or it will seem flat. You can have a garden of all white flowers that will appear pristine and formal, but an all blue garden fades away and looks like it is missing something.

Remember in seventh grade science class, when we weren't staring out the window and daydreaming, we learned about the *cones* and *rods* in our eyes? Cones are the organs of daylight vision. As daylight grows dim, the rod vision is enhanced. Blue is a color of low intensity. It fades in bright sun and appears to increase in intensity as light fades. A bright yellow-green is the point of highest visibility for the eye cones. Blue-grey-green is the point of highest visiblity for the darkness adapted rods.

In the evening garden, the lambs ears, artemesia, and santolina seem to glow. They are good edging plants around a sitting area for night time viewing.

Blues and purples and greens are called "cool" colors, I'm refering to temperature not a synonym for "awesome". Yellows, oranges and reds are warm colors. There is a tendency in our vision for warm colors to advance toward us and for cool colors to recede. Color can appear to change when used in combination with other colors. When green is next to yellow, green is the cooler color. But when that same green is next to blue, it is the warmer color.

When blue is the only flower color in a garden, it will make the area fade into the background. Blue needs an accent or contrast of a different, brighter, warmer color to make it more visually interesting. So when you can't sleep and you're planning your blue garden, make sure you include a color dot of red or yellow or orange to complement the color imagery.

Good plants for the bright accents in the blue garden are red centranthus, maltese cross and cardinal flower. Yellow daylillies, magenta lychnis and orange geum all make the blues stand out more. White is also a good combination color for the blue garden.

Flower colors are caused by biochemical compounds in the plants. Greens are produced by chlorophyll and chloroplastids. Yellows and oranges are created by carotenes and xanthophylls. Anthocyanins give us blue, purple and violet colors in flowers. I'm just crazy about anthocyanin, it makes my favorite flower colors.

Some blue flowers for the spring garden are forget-me-nots, both Spanish and Virginia bluebells, small bulbs like scilla, grape hyacinth, and glory of the snow, blue anenomes, blue columbines, bluets, blue violets and blue pansies. The pale blue flowers of the amsonia blue star, and many shades of blue iris light up a late spring border. Ajuga and periwinkle are good blue groundcovers.

There are lots of blue flowers for the summer garden. Lupin, delphinium, larkspur and cornflower are summer blues. The blue pin cushion *scabiosa* has light blue flowers that catch summer breezes. Blue nigella is also called, love-in-a-mist. Blue morning glories and blue

gentian

clematis are climbing blue flowers.   There are blue butterfly bushes and blue hydrangeas, blue caryopteris, and blue bird hibiscus for woody selections. Blue lobelia and felicia can drape over the edge of a window box.

Tropical agapanthus or plumbago can fill the summer garden with a long season of blue blooms as will the annual blue ageratum. In the summer herb garden, rosemary, borage,   catmint and sage all have blue flowers. There are many veronicas and campanulas with beautiful blue flowers. The large genetian family has glowing blues. Dark blue monkshood flowers stand tall at the end of the summer as do the balloon flower, *platycodon*.

A few years ago, my friend, Elaine, introduced me to the world of blue salvias. Now I'm hooked and the season of blue flowers has been extended well into October and even November. The blue salvias can also be dried for indoor arrangements to last all winter. It's not easy to find the tall annual blue salvias in our local garden centers. I usually get them through mail order. If you grow them from seed, you have to start early. Dark blue, salvia 'indigo spires' had blossoms that can be over a foot long on waving, arching stems. Salvia 'uliginosa', and salvia 'patens' are other splendid blues for the fall garden when it seems that there are only oranges and reds in the Cape Cod landscape, real or imagined.

Cukes

Cucumbers have been cultivated in home gardens for hundreds of years. They have a wide variety of culinary use from soups and salads, to raw or cooked side dishes. And if it weren't for cucumbers, we wouldn't have pickles.

Cucumbers came originally from Southwest Asia where there is no frost. The Latin name for our garden cucumber is *cucumis sativus*. It is in the botanical family *cucurbitaceae* and is cousins with melons, squash and pumpkins.

There are several types of cucumbers and it's not too late this year to plant them. The soil temperature needs to be above 50°F. for cucumbers to thrive and we've had such a long cool spring that cucumbers planted early probably didn't grow much if at all.

When buying seeds, look for varieties that are resistant to insects and diseases. It should say this somewhere on the seed package. Cucumbers are prone to several bacterial and fungal diseases as well as being the select choice of insect pests.

Good soil and site preparation is the greatest defense against cucumber problems. Choose dwarf or compact varieties for container growing in a wooden tub or large pot.

The best way to start cucumbers is by directly seeding where the plant will grow. The tender plants do not transplant well from pots. If you want a little jump start on the growing time, you can presprout the cucumber seeds. Place some seeds between a few layers of damp paper towels and seal in a zip-lock bag. Place on top of the refrigerator (where it is steadily warm) for a day or so until the seeds sprout, then plant them outside carefully. This might save a week outside.

If you have lots of room, you can let the cucumber vines sprawl along the ground. But for limited space, try growing cucumbers up a trellis. Have a sturdy trellis in place at planting time because cucumber plants get very heavy by the end of the season. You may have to lift the young vines up onto the trellis to start them growing vertically. Growing cukes on a trellis keeps the fruit and leaves off the ground and away from soil borne diseases and crawling insects. Harvesting is easier up off the ground.

You can make a timber or wire A-frame trellis that is hinged at the top for flat winter storage. It should be about six feet high with openings large enough for you to reach through and for the fruit to grow easily. Make sure the bottom of the trellis is secured so it won't blow over in a heavy wind.

Choose a sunny spot for growing cukes. They are sun and heat loving plants. Cucumbers are heavy feeders because they grow quickly and need a lot of nutrients. They benefit from weekly feedings of manure or compost tea. To make this "tea" fill a big bucket with water and add cow manure or compost then let it sit and steep for a day. This tea is not for drinking, pour it on the roots of the garden vegetables and flowers.

Cucumbers have male and female flowers for cross pollination. The fruit is produced on the female flowers. You can see the miniature cukes under the petals of the female cucumber flowers. If you cover the young cucumber plants to prevent insect damage, be sure to remove the covers when the flowers start to appear so they can be pollinated by beneficial insects. Otherwise, you'll have to pollinate the flowers with a paintbrush.

Keep the cucumber plants weeded. Weeds compete for nutrients, moisture and light. They also harbor insect pests and diseases. Mulch deeply with straw after weeding.

Radishes and marigolds are good companion plants for cucumbers. Interplant with broccoli and other members of the cabbage family. Early lettuce can be planted before the soil warms up enough for cucumbers.

Watering is crucial for cucumbers. If they do not have enough water, they will be misshapen and bitter. They need at least an inch of water a week. Soaker hoses are good because they wet just the roots. Wet leaves can attract fungal diseases. If your cucumber leaves show signs of disease, do not put them in the compost at the end of the season.

Cucumber beetles are enemies. They are striped or spotted, about 1/4 long and look like elongated lady bugs. Both the larvae and adult stages of the beetles carry plant diseases. They eat the fruit, stems and the leaves of cucumbers. Inspect the plants often for any sign of these pests. Deep mulch and planting disease resistant varieties will help to discourage predation.

Harvest before the cucumbers are fully mature. Pick often while the fruit is dark green. If you let the cukes ripen, get yellow on the end, they will be bitter and the plant will stop making flowers and fruit.

If you've never done it, try making pickles. There are loads of pickle recipes, they make great gifts, go perfectly with summer picnics and they are a great way to use up those billions of cucumbers that can grow on one vine.

Japanese Beetles

June is the month for going on garden tours. There are many of them held in every town on Cape Cod. People open up their gardens to the public for us to see what they've been growing. I think these are a lot of fun.

One of my favorite things to look for in other people's gardens is how plants are combined. There are so many plants that can grow and thrive in our zone that there are almost endless possibilities for mixing colors and shapes in the garden. One of my least favorite things to see in my garden or anyone else's is a Japanese beetle.

I haven't seen any yet this year, but any day now, we should start to see Japanese beetles in Cape Cod gardens. It is one of the most destructive garden pests in Massachusetts and all of the Northeast.

The Japanese beetle, Popillia japonica, is a very colorful insect 1/4 to 1/2 inch long. The wing covers are a shiny bronze color and the area behind the head is a metallic green or blue-green. There are tiny tufts of white hairs along the sides of the abdomen.

The adult stage (beetle) has been reported to feed on over 300 species of plants. Trees, vines, shrubs, fruit, vegetables and ornamental plants are all vulnerable to the chewing Japanese beetle. They can strip a plant leaving only the veins of leaves. They especially like buds and leaves of roses and grape leaves, and can rapidly defoliate entire plants. They often work in groups and feed during the daylight hours.

The larvae of the Japanese beetles are dirty white grubs up to 3/4 of an inch long. If you dig around in your lawn area, you will probably find some. They are generally bent into a "C" shape and have a brown head.

The larvae feed on grass roots and can damage a lawn. They can cause irregular patches of dead or wilted grass in the spring and again in the fall. Turf may be torn up by crows, skunks, raccoons and other birds and animals searching for the grubs to eat.

Japanese beetle larvae overwinter deep in the soil. In the spring when the soil warms up, they move closer to the surface and begin eating the roots of grass and other plants. They pupate in May and June and emerge as adult beetles in late June or early July. At the end of the summer, the beetles burrow under the grass and lay eggs.

The eggs hatch into larvae in the fall and tunnel deep to avoid freezing. Japanese beetles live one to two years.

The Japanese beetle was accidentally introduced into this country in 1916 from guess where? That's right, from Japan. For over eighty years, it has flourished until it is now one of our prime garden pests.

In 1933, government entomologists (bug scientists) isolated a bacterial organism that produces a disease that is fatal to the larval stage of the Japanese beetle. It was called milky spore disease because it brings about an abnormal white color in the insects. In Japan, this is found naturally in the soil and the beetles there are kept to lower numbers.

Milky spore is available at garden centers. It is spread across the lawn and kills the grubs of Japanese beetles and other beetle grubs. Milky spore is harmless to beneficial insects, earthworms, bees, the soil, animals and humans. The spore does not, however, survive freezing and has to be reapplied every year. Application can be any time the ground is not frozen.

For control of the adult beetles, do not use Japanese beetle traps unless everyone in your area is using them. The traps have chemicals to attract the beetles but not all of the many, many beetles that arrive go into the trap. Tests have shown that plants within 30 feet of the traps have higher predation by Japanese beetle than areas without traps.

There are sprays to use on your favorite plants to repel the Japanese beetle. Read the spray label at the garden center to make sure that Japanese beetle is listed because many sprays do not affect them. Most of these should not be used on fruits and vegetables. Floating, fabric covers can protect edible plants when the beetles are out. Hand picking is an effective, if laborious, method of eradication of the beetles. Take a coffee can with some dishwashing or laundry liquid detergent in it and drop the beetles into it. Be quick if you try to squash the beetles with your fingers, feet or trowel because they are good at escaping.

Japanese beetles do not eat geraniums or tansey so you can try planting them near your favorite roses to repel them. Larkspur is supposed to poison Japanese beetles. The pretty blue larkspur might be nice near the roses too. Maybe we'll see some combinations like this on one of the garden tours. With some luck, the public will get to go through the gardens before the Japanese beetles do.

July

Gladiolus

The gladiolus was an acquired taste for me. I used to think of them as funeral flowers only good for large, pastel colored arrangements in remembrance baskets. But I've grown to appreciate the tall, showy, richly hued bloomers, both in the garden and in an arrangement.

Originally from Africa, the gladiolus was found as far north as the Mediterranean, but the greatest concentration of this wild growing flower was in South Africa. The original species has gone through much hybridization to get to the flower that we grow today.

The name *gladiolus* comes from the Latin for "little sword" referring to its leaves. The word "gladiator" comes from the same base. There are currently thousands of named cultivars of gladiolus.

Gladiolus is in the botanical family *iridaceae* and is cousins to the iris and crocus. It is grown from a corm. Corms resemble true bulbs in appearance and many times the words "bulb" and "corm" are used interchangeably when referring to the gladiolus. The main difference between a corm and a bulb can be seen when you cut one of them open.

A true bulb (tulip, daffodil, lily, hyacinth) has layers of food-storing scales surrounding a tiny flower formed during the previous season. A corm (gladiolus, crocus) is a solid fleshy mass; a reservoir of stored energy without an embryonic flower inside. The corm produces leaves and flowers from growth buds at the top of the corm. They reproduce by forming new corms called cormlets or cormels (sounds like a name for those little ears of corn and brown chewy candy).

Gladioli have large, splendid flowers that come in a wide variety of forms and all colors except blue. There are miniatures, doubles, dragons, butterflies, exotics and novelties in standard and giant types. The plants grow from two to six feet tall.

The large types were first developed in 1850 for improved colors, forms and size. They are easily grown from Canada to Florida with a short time from planting to flowering of 70 to 90 days. For the very patient, gladiolus can be grown from seed.

One of the gladiolus' assets is that it really needs minimal attention - good soil preparation, keep weed free and stake to prevent wind damage. Cape Cod soil, if amended with organic matter (manure, compost) should be just right. Remove weeds that compete for nutrients. Use bamboo stakes and string to keep the top-heavy plants erect.

Most gladiolus failures come from not enough water. They need lots of water, enough to keep the soil steadily moist, not a soggy swamp, but damp to the touch. For a dry July and August, use soaker hose or make sure you get out there and water.

Plant in the middle or rear of the mixed border or in an area by themselves after all
danger of frost. Add some superphosphate to the soil at planting
time.Plant pointed side up 3 to 6
inches deep. Some people
plant them much deeper saying
that the plants need less
staking this way. Gladiolus need
to be planted in full sun. They
can be planted very close
together, but at least six inches
apart is better for air circulation
between plants to discourage
fungal diseases.

Plant successively every two weeks to have a long cutting season. Leave the leaves and cut just the flower stems (at an angle) if you want to reuse the corms next year. Cut off some leaves for arrangements if you want to treat the corms like annuals and buy new ones each year.

The blossoms open from the bottom up, cut when the first two start to open.

Lift the corms for storage after the first frost or when the leaves start to turn yellow. Let them cure for a week or so in a dry, airy place then cut off the leaves just above the corm and store until next spring in a place where they won't freeze or be too hot, such as an unheated basement. Discard any bruised or diseased corms. You can peel off the brown, outer layer before planting. The cormlets that have formed can be broken off and planted on their own. They should be big enough to flower in two years.

Plant gladiolus under a *gypsophila* baby's breath plant or *dictamus* gas plant for good companions. It's not too late to put some in this year! There is also a winter hardy gladiolus called *gladiolus callianthus* or "peacock orchid". It grows 2 to 3 feet tall and has white flowers with a dark throat.

Planting Trees

July rhymes with hot'n'dry. It's a better time for harvesting and entertaining than gardening. Did the weed grass get as tall in everyone else's flower beds this year? What a task it is to pull it out. Next year I'll tackle that earlier. Right.

There are many easy garden chores for July. Probably, the most important job is watering. Garden plants do better with regular and thorough watering rather than waiting for forecasted rain that never makes its way over the Cape Cod Canal. Morning is a better time to water than evening because foliage will have a better chance to dry out during the day. When left wet overnight, leaves are more susceptible to fungal spores and diseases.

Mulch helps to retain the moisture in the soil for a little longer, but make sure the much isn't so thick that the water never reaches the roots. A two or three inch thick mulch is enough. Seaweed makes a great mulch.

If you're willing to water, July is a good time to plant a new tree or shrub. There is still a long growing season ahead and trees and shrubs in nursery pots will not be as pot-bound as they will in the fall. Before you fall in love and buy something at the nursery, find out what the plant's mature size will be. To save yourself some headache and expense later, don't plant something right next to the house or driveway that will have to be heavily pruned or moved in a few years.

When you get your beloved new tree or shrub home, give it a good drink of water. Fill the pot to the brim with water, let it drain out and then repeat. Also wet all the leaves because they can dry out easily in transport and not recover.

The current recommendation is not to doctor up the soil too much when you plant trees and shrubs. Research shows that when too much good stuff like compost, peat, and manure is added to the hole, the new tree's roots will not move out into the surrounding soil. The nutrients in the planting hole are used up quickly and the tree or shrub will not be well-anchored by spread out roots. This tree can topple over in a good wind. Add some superphosphate granules to the soil to promote root growth in existing soil.

Dig a hole that is wide and shallow, one that is at least two to three times wider than the container. Most trees and shrubs send out their roots horizontally so you don't have to dig a deep hole, just a wide one. Loosen and moisten the surrounding soil to give the new roots room to wiggle and grow.

The soil level should be just where the roots fan out from the trunk. Many problems occur when trees and shrubs are planted too deeply. Stake only if the plant leans to one side or is top heavy. If there is a steady wind that is going to blow the tree or shrub right over, maybe it's not the right site. Remove all ties and stakes after one year to avoid damage to the bark and wood. Also, take off any wrap that may have come around the trunk of the new tree. Tremendous heat can build up under there and injure the plant.

Mulch a two foot area around the tree to keep down weeds, reserve moisture and protect from the lawn mower and trimmer. Keep the mulch away from the trunk of the tree or shrub.

When the mulch is piled high against the trunk and bark, there are many harmful things that can happen to your woody landscape plants. The tree or shrub can send out new roots into the mulch and not get the nutrients or moisture that are in the soil.

High mulch is the perfect living and hiding place of insects and small rodents that love to chew on bark. The tips of branches and tops of trees will start to drop leaves and die off because they are not getting enough moisture to the roots and up through the tree.

When a big pile of mulch is scraped away from a tree or shrub, there are often open wounds on the bark which are a ideal place for insects and disease to do their work. Okay, I'm not going to start the Mulch Police or anything.

Water is crucial for the new tree and shrub. Every day is not too much. Don't fertilize a newly planted tree for the first year because it needs to make good roots first then upper growth after it can be well supported. Spray the leaves with the water hose to keep off insects. A lot of times a good blast with the hose can do more for a tree or shrub than a spray from any can.

Beach Plums

The fruit of the beach plum should be ready for harvesting in a few weeks. With the very dry summer that we've been having, it's a good thing that the beach plum is so drought tolerant.

Named in 1785 by plant taxonomist, Humphrey Marshall, Prunus maritima, the beach plum has a long history on Cape Cod. It has been used as a food source from pre-colonist times to the present. The beach plum is found growing wild in many places along the Atlantic coast from Maritime Canada to North Carolina. It is abundant on Cape Cod, found growing wild near both the bay and ocean beaches.

Beach plum shrubs are easy to overlook in the wild landscape. Growing from 4 to 15 feet tall, the shrub is most noticeable in the spring (usually May) when it is covered with white flowers along dark branches. The small, oval or round fruit is usually 1/2 to 1 inch long. The color of the fruit, which is ripe in August or early

September, varies from reds to blue-purples. An occasional yellow-fruited shrub can be found in the wild.

The taste of the fruit can be acidic and bitter or mellow and sweet. It can be eaten raw, but the beach plum is mainly harvested for use in jams, jellies and liqueurs. There is a large seed in the middle of the fruit and it takes a lot of picking to get enough fruit for a good batch of jelly.

Since the 1800's, several attempts have been made to produce improved cultivars of our wild growing beach plum shrub for commercial and home use. Barnstable County Cooperative Extension in conjunction with Coonamessett Farm in Falmouth is currently doing a large research project to expand the limited knowledge of the beach plum with the ultimate goal of using the fruit for commercial production. This is being funded by the Massachusetts Dept. of Food and Agriculture through an Agro - Environmental Technology Program. It is in its second year.

The beach plums that are collected from the wild are not reliable from year to year so studies are being conducted that hopefully will result in innovative ideas for increased yield.

There are five sites from Falmouth to Orleans where beach plums are being propagated and evaluated with assistance from a Cornell graduate student, and many local people.

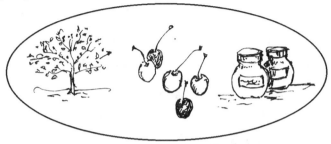

Beach plums can be grown in the Cape Cod home landscape equally as well as those grown on the dunes. Increased soil fertility, however, sometimes results in fewer fruit. I planted some here in 1991 and have not had any fruit yet, nice structure, great leaves, a few blossoms, but no fruit. There is little information available for home landscape possibilities and cultural practices for this rugged, long lived shrub.

The beach plum is not easily transplanted from the wild (also illegal unless it's your own wild land). It has a combination of wide spreading, fibrous roots and a very deep tap root that does not move well. Nursery grown plants that are propagated from named and unnamed varieties are available. The best time to plant is in the early spring. Plant in full sun. The beach plum is salt and drought tolerant.

There are dwarf and common forms of the adaptable beach plum shrub which is a cousin to the cherry and large fruited plum. The beach plum is subject to the same insects and diseases as it's cousins but it generally is a strong, healthy plant. Some of the varieties available are named after Cape Cod towns - 'Eastham' and 'Cotuit'. In a catalog that I have from a nursery in Oregon they describe it as a carefree, architectural exotic shrub with delightful, edible fruit. Not so exotic on Cape Cod.

A group is being organized for people interested in the advancement of the beach plum through the Barnstable County Cooperative Extension Program. "The Cape Cod Beach Plum Growers Association" is forming, or should I say reforming. A group with the same name was active in the 1940's and 50's on Cape Cod. They even produced a label that was used on jars of jam that said the product was "certified" by them. The new group will meet to share information about the plant and its fruit.

The Extension office would be interested to hear from members of the former group and also to see if anyone has a "certified" label from the beach plum group in their barn or attic. The jam inside the jar has probably gone by.

Blackspot

July can be a time of garden woes: bugs, fungus, heat, drought, not enough color, small fruit, big weeds. This is the time when the mistakes we made in the spring become evident. Instead of building a new entry way to the house so you don't have to walk past your pathetic little patch of garden, try some new or different methods for problem prevention.

If the only color in your garden now is orange, green or brown, take a short drive to see what's flowering in other people's gardens. Nurseries and garden centers are a great place to visit in July - no crowds, good bargains, plants blooming and sales people who have time to talk. Fill in some of those spaces in the flower and vegetable gardens with an exciting new cultivar, it might even come back next year.

Make sure you inspect all plants that you buy for any signs of insects or disease before you bring them home. Look under the leaves and along the stems. Why import problems into our gardens when they're already stressed from lack of rain.

There are many varieties of roses that are still at the peak of their bloom in July. Roses along a split rail fence are part of the Cape Cod scene that is remembered by tourists. Most of those old hardy ramblers are resistant to the diseases that plague the hybrid teas which have been bred for their large gorgeous blooms.

Blackspot *Diplocarpon rosae* is probably the most common and most serious of the diseases that affect roses on Cape Cod. The name comes from the small to large circular blackspots that appear on the leaves. The spots may run together to form large, black blotches. When the leaves are severely affected, they turn yellow and then fall off. In humid conditions, some rose plants can become completely defoliated and die.

Many first time rose planters give up after a year or two when their roses die from blackspot. So far, there is nothing that "cures" blackspot, only methods of prevention. There are many fungicide chemicals available at the garden centers and these are often recommended by places where you buy roses.

There are other methods of preventing blackspot that you also might want to try. Roses are not for gardeners who only want to plant and water. They require the benevolent touch of the gardener more than many other plants.

Before you buy a rose plant, look for disease resistant cultivars. You can learn how to choose these plants from the garden section of the library or by attending a group like a Rose Society.

When selecting a site for a rose garden, and most all other kinds of gardens, choose a place where there is full sun and plenty of air circulation. Try to plant on flat land or on a south facing slope, not at the bottom of a slope or in a hollow.

The president of the Lower Cape Rose Society, recommends that you remove any damaged leaves on rose plants and keep the garden clean. Keep water off the lower foliage and water early to give the leaves a good chance to dry off during the day. You can try using a non-toxic product like Ultra Fine Horticultural Oil as a spray instead of the usual fungicides. This puts a protective layer of oil on the rose leaves making it very difficult for the fungal spores of blackspot to attach. It should be applied every five days for continual protection.

So far this method of blackspot prevention has not been officially recommended by the American Rose Society or the manufacturers of the Horticultural Oil, but it will not hurt you, your roses nor your environment to try it. Some gardeners have also had success against blackspot by spraying the rose leaves with a solution of baking soda and water (one tablespoon baking soda / one gallon water).

Don't give up on the roses or the rest of the garden. It's only July. Once in a while it rains in August. Until then we can water, visit better gardens or go away on vacation, just like a tourist.

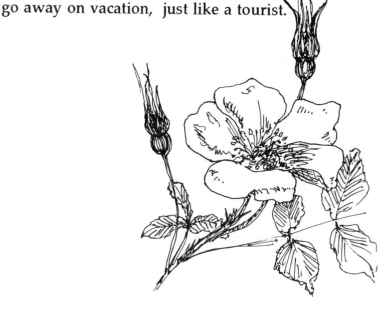

August

Hydrangeas

Have you seen all the big blue mop-head hydrangeas this year? Wow! They were looking a little droopy in mid July, but after we finally got a little rain they stood back up. Many are still giving a nice long performance of bloom.

The hydrangea family is a very big one. There is a garden in France that has over 600 different, named cultivars. The big blue, pink or purple flowering shrub that we see all over Cape Cod are called, *Bigleaf Hydrangea* or *Hydrangea macrophylla*. This *macrophylla* group is further broken down into two groups: the mop-heads which are called *hortensias* and the ones with the flat sprays of blossoms called *lacecaps*. The botanical terms are *globosus* for the mop-heads or globe shaped flowers and *corymbosus* for the broad or flat shaped flower clusters. The name *hydrangea* comes from the Greek word for water.

Sometimes, the name *hortensia* is used interchangeably with *hydrangea* to further confuse the wee gardener. Hydrangeas are most closely related to the mock orange or *philadelphus* shrub.

Bigleaf hydrangeas were collected from the wild in China in the 1780's by English botanist and plant explorer, Sir Joseph Banks. He also collected tree peonies on the same trip. Bigleaf hydrangeas are also native to Japan and other parts of Asia. Some of the white flowering hydrangeas are native to the southern parts of America.

Over 200 years of hybridization and cultivation have gone into the large flowering shrubs that we grow today. Hydrangea marcophylla is now a long lived, disease and pest resistant shrub that needs minimal care to thrive. We are at the northern reach of the planting zone for the bigleaf hydrangea. People further North than us can plant most of the white flowering cultivars (pee gee, oak leaf, climbing) but the blue, pink and purple flowering varieties cannot tolerate winter temperatures below zero °F.

The flowers of the bigleaf hydrangea are very unusual because they can change color according to the pH of the soil. Cape Cod soil is generally acidic, reading somewhere in the 5's. This is a good pH for blue flowers on hydrangea macrophylla.

If you take that same blue hydrangea, dig it up, mix in 1 lb. lime to 3 sq. ft. of soil, then replant the shrub, the flower should be pink the next year. Conversely, you can mix 1 lb. aluminum sulfate to 3 sq. ft. soil to change a pink flowering variety to blue. This is not an exact science and should be only tried for fun. Too much lime can cause mottled leaves and other problems. White flowering varieties of hydrangea will not change color with pH manipulation.

If your hydrangea has nice healthy leaves and no flowers it is probably caused by one of five reasons:

1. too much shade - move to a brighter location
2. over-fertilization - lightly fertilize in early spring only
3. winter damage - buds are formed in the fall for next springs blossoms, very cold temps. can destroy flower buds and not harm leaf buds
4. summer or fall too hot - not much we can do about that, buds won't set if temps are too high
5. most frequently why hydrangeas don't bloom - improper pruning.

Pruning is an art with the bigleaf hydrangea. For new plants, do not prune at all for the first few years except to take out very dead wood. Then if you want to keep the shrub vigorous, cut out some of the oldest canes to encourage new growth.

This should only be done right after bloom time in August. The flower buds for the next year form right after bloom time so they should not be cut off. They look like asparagus tips and can easily be mistaken for leaf buds. When pruning out old canes, cut them just a few inches up from the ground, not half way up the stem.

It is very easy to increase your hydrangea collection by propagation. If you try to grow hydrangea from seed, you might get a different plant from the parent because of hybridization. Cuttings and divisions should result in true offspring. For division, just take a sharp spade or shovel and cut off a rooted section of the hydrangea and move it someplace else.

To propagate by cuttings, find a leafy stalk with no flowers; cut it off with three sets of leaves. Remove the lower two leaf sets and then lay the cutting on the ground next to the parent plant and bury the stem leaving the top leaves above the soil. By next spring you should have nicely rooted cuttings to move on to a pot or another garden location. Easy, easy. No hormones, no grow lights, no special soil.

Just be careful that you don't lose your rooted cuttings in the spring when you rake away the winter mulch like I did. Dang. Will try again next fall.

Blueberries

W hen I was young (after dinosaurs, before Elvis) my grandmother would say, "if you can pick enough blueberries, I'll make you a pie". Between her cottage and the lake there was a white pine forest where the understory was covered with lowbush blueberries. I remember filtered sunlight, the smell of pine needles, tiny blue berries and a great big bowl.

This year, the wild blueberries are on the small side because it has been so dry which means more picking per pie. If you don't have woods with wild ones, you can plant a few bushes of our native American fruit, the blueberry. If rhododendrons or azaleas are doing well near your yard, than you will probably have success growing blueberries because they have similar requirements.

The names *blueberry* and *huckleberry* are often used interchangeably, but they are from two different plant families. This is like saying "Huckleberry Hound" and "Huckleberry Finn" are the same person - no way.

Wild lowbush blueberries do not transplant well to the garden setting unless you can reproduce their growing conditions. It is better to buy potted plants grown for garden cultivation.

Choose a spot in full sun to plant your blueberries. The more shade, the less berries. Most of Cape Cod soil is naturally acidic, but the garden usually has a higher pH for most vegetables and flowers. Blueberries will not produce fruit if the pH is above 5.5. You can make raised beds with acid soil for each blueberry plant or group of plants. Have your soil tested if you're not sure what the pH is.

Some blueberries need cross-pollination to set fruit, so you should plan to buy at least two different varieties. You can choose between lowbush *Vaccinium angustifolium* , highbush *Vaccinium corymbosum,* and even some hybrids that are midheight. Extend the picking season with plants that have early, mid and late ripening times.

Prepare the soil by loosening it and adding some peat moss. Do not add any manure because this can raise the pH. Once the blueberry is planted, the shallow roots should not be disturbed. Cover the roots with a thin layer of soil and a thick (3 to 6 inches) mulch to keep down weeds and keep in moisture.

Use pine needles, oak leaves or sawdust. Fresh sawdust will sometimes rob nitrogen from the soil, so plan to add more nitrogen if you use only this mulch. Add new mulch every year in the spring as the old mulch breaks down. Blueberries do not need much fertilizer. They grow naturally in very poor soil. A little compost mixed in with the mulch should take care of all the nutrient needs.

For the first few years, do not do any pruning except to remove dead wood. In later years, thin out weaker shoots in the center of the plant for better air circulation, and to encourage new growth. The cutting should be done at ground level, not halfway up the stem. Pruning techniques can rejuvenate old blueberry shrubs and keep new ones vigorous.

The blueberry sets fruit on wood grown the previous year. Remember this when pruning so you won't cut off all the fruit. Remove all the suckers (shoots that come up from the roots) except for one or two. Cut off all weak, twiggy branches. Cut off one branch where two are crossed and rubbing together. The best time for pruning is anytime after the leaves have fallen off in late fall, and before new growth starts in the spring.

In the spring, blueberry buds look like single swollen points on the branches. Each swollen bud will produce many flowers and then many berries. Cut off buds at the ends of branches to leave only 3 to 5 buds per stem. If you leave on all the buds, the blueberries will be smaller.

Harvest blueberries when they are fully ripe. Taste test a few before you pick them all. Blueberries will not ripen more after they are picked. Wait until they're ready. The birds and chipmunks, however, will not wait and you have to cover the plants with strong netting to keep them out. Some people drape the plants with nets and some have structures with wire or nets attached. Blueberries are pollinated by bees and other insects so remove nettings at blossom time so they can get in there.

Blueberries are long lived plants that are generally pest and disease free. Sticky red balls are available at the garden centers to hang in the garden. These attract and catch many of the insects that attack blueberries. You can reuse these traps by washing them in the fall and applying petroleum jelly and tanglefoot which is available at garden centers or through mail order in the spring.

Recommended reading for this topic is "Blueberries For Sal" by Robert McCloskey. Then you can go out to gather the fruit, make a pie and make a memory.

August Chores

I f you love having a garden, you've found out that there are always chores and maintenance to keep it going. There are lots of things to do in August to finish off the season and get ready for next year which of course will be better than this year. We gardeners are optimists. We believe that little seeds can become fruit.

This is the time to think about spring, or at least about early spring flowers. It's time to get out that pile of bulb catalogs and place your order. You can wait to buy bulbs at the local nurseries next month, but the ones that you really want disappear fast. Mail order is more reliable for unusual varieties.

It's hard to think about pastel colored tulips when you're looking at a bed of black-eyed susans but you'll be glad you made the effort next spring. If you don't have any bulb catalogs, ask a gardening friend for some. If you still can't find any, look in the back of any gardening magazine for addresses and telephone numbers of bulb companies. Read the catalog descriptions carefully.

Some companies offer bulbs at very low prices, but these bulbs can be very small and not flower for years. Look for top size bulbs when ordering.

If you had good geraniums or coleus this year, now is a good time to take stem cuttings to reproduce those plants next year. They will root quickly and form some sizable plants by winter. Choose stems without flowers for best rooting and cut off some pieces about 5 inches long. Remove the leaves from the lower portion of the stem cutting then put it into a pot filled with moist sand, vermiculite (available at the garden centers) or potting mix. Bring them inside and place near a sunny window. You can keep your beautiful geraniums and coleus going for years with this method.

Fill up some spaces in the vegetable garden by planting lettuce and even radish if they can get some shade when we have very hot days. When you pick onions from the garden, let them sit in the sun to cure for a day or two and they will store better. The strawberries are sending out runners now. Take the runners and pin them on top of a small pot filled with soil. Keep the runners connected to the mother plant until they make good roots - a few weeks at least. Then cut and move them to a new garden, or give some to friends for planting. If you don't want to move the runners,they should be cut off to prevent overcrowding.

This is a good time to make up a nursery bed if you don't have one. It doesn't have to be very big, just a few square feet. It is a good place to heel in plants that you bought (because you couldn't resist, because they were on sale, because you always wanted them) until you have a place to put them. You can start a lot of cuttings here from your own garden or from friends. You'll appreciate it next spring when it's time to buy lots of plants again.

Now is a good time to plant pansy and columbine seeds. They will germinate quickly and the little plants will be large enough to move this fall. Then they will only need some mulch put over them after the ground is chilled in December. You should get nice early blossoms from them next spring.

Keep a lookout for the caterpillars called   tomato hornworms.   They eat pepper   plants, tomato plants and eggplants   too. They can defoliate a plant   and ruin the fruit   in quick t i m e .   They   are hard to detect because of their green coloring.   When you see   one you'll know how it got the name "hornworm".   There is a single,   horn-like

143

projection sticking out at the back of the caterpillar. These are bad bugs. Pick them off the plants and put them into a container of soapy water. Some people like to squish them. There are probably some little boys in your neighborhood who will volunteer for this garden chore.

August is when you should stop watering your amaryllis plant if you want to have it bloom inside this winter. It is also the time to get out your hand trowel and dig out the rooted shoots of invasive plants in the garden before they come back next year and take over. This includes *monarda* bee balm, mints, loosestrife, and many others. Just take a look out there - you'll see what's been spreading out too much.

I was looking through an old English garden magazine and saw a photo of a raised bed garden up on wooden legs. It was planted with different kinds of thyme with a sundial in the center. They called it a Thyme Table. Don't you just love a garden pun? Remember to water the garden deeply in the morning and order those spring bulbs. I will if you will.

Xeriscape

Last summer when there was plenty of rain, I put in a new perennial border in a place that is hard to get at to water. This fall, I'm going to take every droopy plant out of that garden and replace it with a xerophyte. I should have known better, and planned for seasons without rain.

Xeriscaping is the popular term for landscaping to save water. With good planning, it can also mean low maintenance gardening. The Greek root word *xeros* for *dry* should not be mixed up with the word *xerox* for *corporate copy*. Xerophytes are plants that do well in dry conditions. The letter "x" is pronounced like a "z" in zero for these words.

A xeriscape is not a dry and barren landscape with a few cactus plants, parched gravel and maybe an old cow skull. Xeriscaping is simply using a waterwise plan that includes plants that adjust to low water conditions. This kind of gardening can be adapted to fit almost any garden style because there are so many drought tolerant plants from which to choose. This past summer has been a lesson for us to see which of our plants stand up to drought conditions.

There are whole books about xeriscaping at the bookstores and libraries that include long lists of plants and trees that are suitable for this type of landscaping. Many plants listed are common and easy to find at Cape Cod garden centers.

The best place to start with a xeriscape plan is the soil. Good soil structure holds water better and longer for plant availability. This can be accomplished by loosening up the garden soil and adding compost and well rotted manure to the top 10 to 12 inches. Organic matter should be added to any garden every year in the spring because plants use up a lot of nutrients in the soil during the growing season.

Where possible, the areas of lawn should be reduced to save watering. Turf has a high water requirement to maintain that nice green color - about an inch of rainfall a week. We didn't get an inch of rain for the whole month of July this year. Planting groundcovers and seeding with more drought tolerant grass seeds can help to reduce water usage in drought times. A xeriscape garden doesn't have to be a waterless garden.

A garden pool or other water feature can take up lawn space and use comparatively less water than frequent irrigation.

After site and soil preparation comes the fun part of xeriscape - choosing the plants. There are xeriscape plant lists available at the County Extension office in Barnstable or you can just start by asking someone at the local garden centers which plants are suitable for the low water landscape.

Plants that are appropriate for the xeriscape plan have developed clever ways to survive in drought conditions. Spines and thorns in plants like cactus and thistles keep marauders away from their juicy stems, trap moisture and help to shade the plant as well. There are plants with small or very narrow leaves to cut down on surface for minimal moisture loss in dry and windy areas. The familiar broom shrubs, lavender, queen-anne's-lace, and thread leaf coreopsis are examples of this.

There are many kinds of fuzzy, grey leafed plants to choose from for the xeriscape plan. This kind of leaf deflects strong sunlight and conserves moisture by trapping it in the hairy surface. Lamb's ears, santolina, dusty miller and some of the sages are examples of this.

Succulent and fleshy leaves such as those of sedums conserve and retain moisture through times of drought. You'll notice that old reliable sedum 'Autumn Joy' is doing just fine even if it wasn't watered all summer. Swordlike leaves and rosette shapes of plants like yucca, funnel any moisture down toward the roots. Bearded iris, peonies and day lilies are more drought tolerant because of leaf shape and their moisture retaining fleshy root systems.

After you've chosen your waterwise plants, they will need some extra moisture the first season until they can become established in their new home. This seems contrary to xeriscape principals, but the roots need help through water and nutrients to get a good start for later strength. It's easy to forget that all plants are living, growing organisms. With a little help, xerophytes are plants that can flourish even in a parched Cape Cod summer.

September

Chrysanthemum

hrysanthemum is a good word for a spelling bee. A good word and a great plant. By now, all the garden centers have out their colorful displays of this popular fall bloomer.

Chrysanthemums have a long horticultural history. They were cultivated in China, Japan and other Asian countries for centuries before they were collected by Europeans. I recently got a book from the library called, *Plant Hunters* by Alice Coats. It is a chronicle of the intrepid plant explorers and collectors from the 1500's to the 1900's. Heady stuff. Very "Indiana Jones" type perilous adventures to find new plants and flowers for science and gardens. Chrysanthemums were mentioned often as a popular subject of collecting.

In the 1800's, there were many flower shows just for the presentation of fancy "mum" hybrids. Some of these huge, showy blossoms were far from their wild ancestors in appearance. The flower still has an avid following today. There are a lot of chrysanthemum web sites.

The chrysanthemum family is a very large one. In the past few years, taxonomists have changed the Latin identifying names for many of the mums, but the common names are still the same for easier identification. Chrysanthemums are classified and named by their flower forms and by the time of year when they bloom.

The name *chrysanthemum* comes from the Greek words for golden flowers: "chrysos" and "anthos". In Japan, there is a Chrysanthemum festival in October. In Florida, you can see more chrysanthemums than you would ever believe at Cypress Gardens. If you're lucky, you might even get to see a stack of water skiers too.

After centuries of hybridization, there are thousands of named cultivars from which to choose. Some familiar cousins in the chrysanthemum family are: painted daisy, marguerites, feverfew, nippon or Montauk daisy, and shasta daisy. The potted chrysanthemums that are at the garden centers now are commonly called hardy garden mums.

The hardy garden chrysanthemums can continue to bloom for many weeks if they are given a little attention. They come in may rich colors and flower forms from the tiny "button" flowers that are less than an inch across to the larger rounded "pom poms".

There are singles, doubles, spoons, cushions, spikes, dwarfs, giants and other amusing names to describe the flower shapes. When looking for a chrysanthemum to buy, it will not be easy to choose.

After you've narrowed down the colors and the flower forms that you're attracted to, check the plant over for health and vigor. Also look for insects and any sign of mold or mildew. Probably the most important thing is to feel the potting soil to see if it has some moisture. A dry mum is not a happy mum. This goes for mums in the garden too. Give plenty of water but stop before making the soil soggy.

When you bring the mums home you can put them in the garden, in the house, into new containers, or into flower boxes that might be a little drab by September. Chrysanthemums go great with fall asters, flowering kale, and many of the leaf shapes of flowers that have gone by. They look terrific in baskets on a porch or deck or in an entry way. They will last longer if they get some plant food and enough water. Most can take some light frost and keep on blooming.

Chrysanthemums make wonderful cut flowers because they last a long time and their stems are stiff enough for arranging. To make them last longer in water, slit the stems up from the bottom for about an inch. Also soak the bottom of the stem in an inch of water that has just come to a boil to scald it. This keeps the stems stiff longer, even if it sounds like a cruel thing to do. Change the vase water daily and add a little sugar.

You can put hardy mums into the garden soil when you get them home but they will need a LOT of maintenance next spring and summer if you want to get the magnificent show of bloom that comes from the potted plants from nurseries. It can be done with pinching, pruning, disbudding, covering, thinning and hoping for the best. If you just plant and ignore them, they will probably spread out into your garden and have leggy stems with sparse, small blooms. Dwarf and single forms seem to do better for repeat performance. A lot of manual labor goes into those beautiful potted plants.

If you're keeping the chrysanthemums in pots remember to water them often, even if we get rain. Once they dry out, the blossoms start turning brown and falling off. Now, all together, let's spell "chrysanthemum".

Spinach

What's green, leafy, loaded with vitamins and minerals including the currently oft recommended calcium, and is a major player in an old cartoon? That's right, Spinach. This is a good time to plant spinach in the garden for eating this fall. Later on, spinach can be planted in a cold frame or other protected area for fresh eating all winter.

There are a few kinds of spinach seeds available for gardening here. There is regular Spinach *Spinacia oleracea*, New Zealand Spinach *Tetragonia expansa* which is heat and drought tolerant for our summer gardens, Malabar Spinach or Indian Spinach *Basella alba* which is a vine, and Oriental spinach which has a spinach taste but is a different edible leafy plant.

Regular spinach likes the cooler, medium light days of spring and fall. If planted in the hot dry summer, it will bolt or quickly go to seed.

New Zealand spinach is a better choice for the summer garden. Indian and oriental spinach are better grown in the spring and summer garden also.

Spinach has been cultivated in food gardens for centuries. It's origins are traced back to wild growing plants in Eurasia in the area of what is now around Iran. The Latin name for spinach comes from the word for spiny or prickly, referring to the seed covering. It is in the Goosefoot Family of botanical classification and is closely related to beets.

You don't need a very large area for growing spinach. It doesn't have to be planted in rows. It can even be grown in a container like a 1/2 barrel if that's all the room you have. Clear an area in the garden where something else like beans, peas or cukes has finished off. Toss the old plants onto the compost pile unless they are diseased and prepare the soil for the spinach.

Loosen up and turn over the soil with a garden fork. It shouldn't need to be tilled again until next spring. Spinach likes a sweet soil (pH 6 - 7) so add a handful of powered lime before planting. Cape Cod soil is generally acidic so test once or twice a year for pH.

Spinach needs extra nitrogen to make those nice dark green leaves but don't use too much manure in the soil. Studies have shown that too much manure can give spinach an unpleasant taste.

For additional nitrogen use compost or a little commercial fertilizer. On the package labels of all commercial fertilizers there are 3 numbers prominently displayed. The first number stands for nitrogen. Look for a fertilizer with a bigger first number for the spinach patch. Bloodmeal, fish meal or soybean meal are good organic sources for nitrogen. Wear gloves when hand spreading fertilizers and lime.

Spinach is very easy to grow. There are seeds still available at the garden centers for fall planting. Look for packets of 'Bloomsdale', 'Melody' or 'Tyee'. Seed planting is not just for spring. Fall spinach gets planted directly in the garden soil. No need to start in small containers first.

Look for seeds that are resistant to blight and other fungal diseases. Most spinach seeds are chemically treated to prevent damping off during germination. For untreated seeds, mail order is probably the best source. Read the seed packets. Many will say if the variety is good for fall planting.

Plant spinach seeds 1/4 to 1/2 inch deep and keep moist. Water during dry spells. You can cut off the outer leaves as they grow, or you can wait and cut the entire plant at maturity. This is when 6 or more leaves are 6 or so inches long in about 6 weeks. Don't wait too long or the plant will go to seed and be bitter.

Wash quickly after picking to keep in the most vitamins. Fresh spinach should be used within a week of picking. It is a good freezer veggie and it can also be dried. Ooh - spinach frittata, spinach salad, spanakopita.

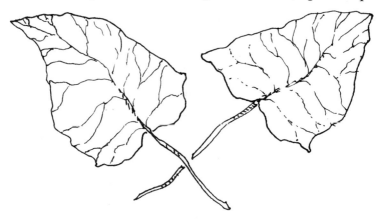

Spinach makes a good companion plant. A friend of mine mixes up different lettuce, spinach, radish, carrot and onion seeds all together and sows them in a 3 foot square raised bed. When the seeds sprout, they need to be thinned with a rake or by hand, and soon there is a salad from a small area that produces for weeks. I'm going to try this mixed up method with left over seeds. If you don't want to combine so many plants, you can try just spinach and radishes, or spinach and lettuce.

But don't plant spinach near sweet peas. The next thing you know, you'll be seeing Popeye or Olive Oyl.

Groundcovers

A well-manicured green lawn is a beautiful part of any property, but it requires a tremendous amount of labor, expense and energy for maintenance in the Cape Cod environment. If you are looking for ways to reduce or replace lawn areas, there are many ground cover plants to choose from that can add beauty and variety to your landscape. Groundcovers are also useful as erosion control for slopes or other hard to mow areas.

Groundcover is a general term used in gardening to describe plants that have a low, spreading habit. It usually refers to plants that are under 2 feet tall, but taller spreading plants like rugosa roses can be used for the same purpose. Groundcovers come with many leaf shapes and textures. Some are grown chiefly for their foliage which includes both deciduous and evergreen species. There are groundcovers with attractive, fragrant flowers and even berries.

The main feature that we look for in ground covers can be considered a bad habit for a plant in a perennial flower bed. For a plant to be successful as a groundcover, it is encouraged to spread. There are groundcovers that expand out in clumps like hosta and day lily. And some spread out by creeping with roots or vining stems like vinca, pachysandra or ivies. There are woody stemmed groundcovers like some junipers or cotoneasters, and ornamental grasses and sedges that are used in this way too.

If you've found that you've turned out to be a plant collector with a variety of unrelated trees and shrubs dotting your landscape, groundcovers are a good way to tie areas together. You can create flowing, low maintenance areas by using long curves of ground covers between two or more architectural elements on your property. This might be good for that sometimes boring stretch between a building and a driveway.

Groundcover areas take longer to establish than a new lawn, but after a few seasons they are usually much easier to maintain. This is a good time of year to think about putting in an area for planting groundcovers. There are still flats and pots of groundcovers at the garden centers and the prices will probably be better than those next spring. It is a good time to help your gardening friends divide up some of their crowded plant areas. You can trade some of your perennials for their spreading groundcovers.

There are still quite a few weeks of growing time for establishing a groundcover area before a hard freeze.

Groundcover areas look more natural if they have a curved shape. Straight lines go well with more formal settings. Unless you are a diligent edger, try to use some sort of barrier between the grass and the groundcover area to save yourself a lot of labor when the grass tries to creep into the groundcover. There are plastic, metal, masonry and wood barriers from which to choose. Many of the new garden edgers are almost invisible when in place.

Pachysandra, *Japanese spurge* and periwinkle, *vinca* are probably the most commonly used ground covers. There are several cultivars in both of these varieties if you want something different. Pachysandra comes in variegated leaf forms and vinca flowers come in white, purples and reds as well as the familiar blues.

If you already have an established pachysandra area, you can rejuvenate it early next spring by going over it with the lawn mover set at the highest blade setting. It should leaf out quickly and look better. If your leaves are looking a little yellowed, it is probably time for some fertilizer in the spring. Don't fertilize now because it could encourage new growth that won't have time to harden off before freezing.

Good groundcovers with fragrant flowers are violets, lily of the valley, some thymes and chamomiles. Some garden centers still have some of the new 'carpet roses' which make great groundcovers with long lasting flowers. The low-growing ajuga comes in different leaf colors including one with pink edges. All ajugas have nice upright flowers in the spring and will quickly form an evergreen carpet. There are many groundcovers that are suitable for shady areas including: foam flower, *tiarella* hostas, ferns, sweet woodruff, and epimedium.

bearberry

You can find long lists of good groundcovers at the County Extension office or at the libraries in the garden section. Look for plants that will be appropriate for average planting Zone 6; and for the conditions on your site - sunny or shade, moist or dry, steep or flat. Groundcovers are by definition plants that spread out. Many can be very invasive when placed in the wrong setting. But if you're looking for a planting, not paving, solution to minimize mowing, groundcovers are for you.

Fall Asters

Blue skies, cooler days, fresh tomato sandwiches, less traffic, asters blooming, what could be better? The fall asters are providing masses of color now in the landscape. They are equally at home in the meadow garden and the formal border. There are wild asters growing on the roadsides and fantastic potted asters at the garden centers.

Fall asters are also called Michaelmas Daisies. This name comes from St. Michael whose festival is celebrated on September 29th when many of the asters are full out. *Aster* comes from the Greek and Latin words for *star* . The flowers remind me more of fireworks than stars. Maybe stars blowing up. They come in many colors - whites, yellows, reds, blues and purples in hazy pastels and brilliant, intense hues (not hughes).

The fall aster family is a very big one. There are low-growing alpine varieties and North American natives that can get up to 10 feet tall. The flowers come in single and double forms. There are so many wild asters that an exact identification of any one cultivar is debatable. Asters hybridize freely in the wild and in the garden. The seed can produce offspring with a different flower color, size and even leaf shape from the parent plant.

Fall asters are in the botanical family *Compositae* which is commonly called the daisy group. The flowers in this plant family are somewhat different from most other flower types. If you have a magnifying glass or very, very good eyes, you can open one up and see the interesting parts of the fall aster. What we commonly think of as one flower is, botanically speaking, many small flowers crowded together on a common receptacle.

You'd think that the aster flower has a lot of petals surrounding a solid round center which is usually yellow. No. There are two kinds of complete flowers that make up each fall aster. There are the many "disk flowers" which are tubular shaped and in the center. And there are the "ray flowers", what we would mistakenly call the petals, which surround the center.

If you look closely you can see all the flower parts and the tiny area that ripen into seed at the bottom on both the ray and disk flowers. Usually, only the disk, or center flowers of compositae flowers produce seed.

The compositae flower heads can be made up of just disk flowers - like thistles, just ray flowers - like dandelions, or of both rays and disks - like sunflowers and fall asters. Just under the "flower" head is a leafy area and a single stem. Or if you wanted to sound really smart, you could say, "the entire head is subtended by an involucre of several to many bracts which are usually leaf-like."

A couple of hundred years ago, plant collectors from Europe came over to North America and gathered our roadside wild asters. They were hybridized, improved, and named in Europe. Today we can buy descendants of these plants in our local garden centers. On the fall aster tags you might see: Aster novae-angliae or Aster nova-belgii followed by a name like 'Alma Potschke'. Nova-angliae is a Latinized word for New England. Nova-belgii is a Latinized word for New York which was previously called New Belgium.

Asters will grow in almost any soil but they will perform best in good, humus-rich garden soil. Plant in full sun. They will tolerate some shade, but there won't be as many flowers. If you want to grow fall asters from seed, start them early - January to February. Seed collected from your plants or from the wild is not reliable for reproducing color or fertility.

If you buy a nice fall aster, you can easily increase it by division until in a few years you almost have too many. Fall asters spread out quickly and can take over a garden area with leggy stems if they are not divided and pinched back. In the late fall, mark where they are planted and divide in spring when the leaves are up - April to May. Take 5 - 10 rooted sections and make a new clump to move somewhere else. Unlike plants grown from seed, the offshoots will flower true to the parent plant. Pinch back once or twice during the growing season - June to July, to make a more compact flowering mass. Some of the taller cultivars need to be staked or you can plant them between some tall perennials whose flowers have already gone by.

Fall asters are good companion plants for coneflowers and autumn sedums. There are fall blooming blue salvias and garden golden-rods *Solidago* that are also compatible. They are good container plants to liven up the front of the house and they make long lasting cut flowers. In *The Language of Flowers* , Michaelmas Daisies stand for "Afterthought". Remember to include them in the next garden plan.

October

Bring in Houseplants

t the time of this writing, we still haven't had a frost. There hasn't been any blackening on the basil plants yet - a sure sign of cold weather. Some people keep their tomato plants going until frost, but I took ours down and cleared off the beds. The green tomatoes can be used for relish, cooked up as is, or saved for later use. The spinach is up. The dahlias still brighten the back border with their profuse bloom.

If you haven't done it already, it's time to start getting those houseplants ready to bring back inside. If you lift them off the patio or deck and just carry them into the house, you'll be asking for trouble in a month or so. While outside they probably picked up some bugs. Start by inspecting the plants. Look under the leaves and along the stems for any signs of insects or disease. Spray with some insecticidal soap or carefully hand clean all surfaces. Discard if there's too much damage.

Another thing that happened to your houseplants when they were outside this summer was that they grew. Maybe a lot. This is a good time to repot.

Repotting can be done outside while it's still warm enough because this is a messy job. If the houseplant was planted in the garden for the summer, it will need some extra care when repotting. The roots have probably spread out quite a bit, so be careful when lifting from the soil so the new roots don't snap off.

Soil renewal helps keep plants vigorous, with resulting better foliage and flowers. Plants use up soil nutrients fairly quickly in a pot. Water can compact the soil and the pH in potting soil can change which makes it difficult for the plants to take up nutrients. Repotting and discarding the old soil can help get rid of insects or their eggs that might have been deposited during their outside summer vacation. Some plants can stay in the same old pot, in the same old soil for years but all house plants can benefit from some new soil. Choose a pot that is just one size bigger.

Large plants growing in big containers can be difficult to repot. Top dressing is a good alternative for these. Scrape away a few inches of the old soil with your hands because metal tools can injure the roots. Adding some new potting soil just to the top area of a big house plant can help put off the job of repotting for another year or so.

You can buy potting soil from the grocery store or at the garden centers. Look for potting mix that is soil based rather that peat based. The peat based soils dry out too fast and do not support the plants as well. There are specialty mixes for certain kinds of plants such as cactus or African violet. Or you can make your own potting soil using one of a number of soil recipes. You can mix in a little superphosphate (which promotes root growth) or a small amount of slow release fertilizer pellets to get the newly potted plant off to a good start. If you can only find peat based potting soils, buy a few different kinds and mix together.

Remember not to use garden soil for indoor plants unless you're willing to sterilize it. Heating to 180°F will destroy everything harmful as well as anything beneficial in the garden soil. If you're planning to use your kitchen oven to sterilize soil, be prepared for unpleasant odors. Cooked soil is not a good smell.

If you have some geraniums, *pelargoniums* that were wonderful this summer and you'd like to keep them for next year, there are a few different ways to overwinter them. If the geraniums were outside in pots, you can just cut them back - to about 4 inches high, strip off the leaves, and put them in a sunny window inside.

They will quickly sprout new leaves. Keep cutting back the stems if they get too leggy. You can also take the geraniums out of the soil or out of the pots and shake off all the soil. Hang them upside down in a dark, dry cellar or attic that stays cool but doesn't freeze. Repot in March, giving them time to sprout before summer.

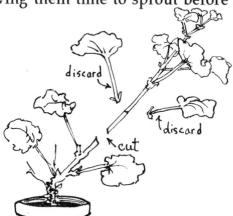

Geraniums, *pelargoniums* are easy to start from cuttings. This is a way to reproduce the plant as well as enjoy the flowers of the parent plant outside right up until frost. Choose a healthy shoot without flowers and count down three or four leaves from the top and then cut. Keep the top two leaves of the cutting and remove the lower leaves. Place the cutting in potting mix and place in a warm sunny window. Keep dry for a week or so then water once a week. You can do a whole flat of cuttings or just one to a pot. Most geranium problems occur from overwatering. Pinch back as needed over the winter to keep the new plants strong and bushy.

Burning Bush

Some plants are grown for their flowers, some for the fruit or the fragrance. Some plants are grown for the food that they make, some, like the cactus for fun. Now it's October and the plants that are featured, are the ones that are grown for fall foliage.

If you're going East on Rte. 6A in Brewster, look at the edge of the field across from Millstone Road. The rich scarlet foliage of the dozen or so burning bushes *Euonymus elata* is at the peak now. *Elata* is from botanical Latin for *winged*. The burning bush is also known as winged euonymus. Many other trees and shrubs have beautiful color at this time of year, but the burning bush can be depended on, no matter what the climate brought the preceding season, for spectacular reds in the fall landscape.

The burning bush is part of the large Euonymus family. There are other deciduous and evergreen Euonymus shrubs, creeping Euonymus vines, and even Euonymus trees including one called *Wahoo*.

Mostly native to Asia, the Euonymus have been widely distributed and are now naturalized all over North America. Euonymus is in the botanical family *Celastraceae* . It is closely related to the ubiquitous bittersweet vine. If you look at the seed pods of both the bittersweet vine and the burning bush, you will see the resemblance.

The derivation of the common name *burning bush* is obvious in the fall. It gets its Latin name *Euonymus elata* from the corky *wings* that protrude along the branches. These winged branches are great for arrangements and for winter interest after the leaves fall off. The name, Euonymus, was taken from Greek mythology. Eunoyme was the mother of the Furies.

Back here on Cape Cod, the winged euonymus is easily grown in sun or part shade. It tolerates a wide range of soils and even some salt spray. It can be grown as a hedge or as a specimen plant. You can plant a burning bush now or in the spring. The air is getting cooler, but the soil is still warm enough to plant.

The burning bush is not recommended as a foundation plant unless you want to be trimming and pruning. It will get too big (up to 20 feet) next to the house unless you can find a variety with the word 'Compacta' at the end of the name.

The Euonymus elata 'Compacta' can get up to 8 feet tall; it has the same foliage and form as its taller relative but it doesn't have wings on the branches.

Late winter/early spring is the best time for pruning or shearing the burning bush. The dense twiggy foliage takes clipping well. It can be shaped into topiary or as a formal hedge. A container grown winged euonymus can be made into Bonsai. But the way I like best to see a burning bush is out in the landscape with its large spreading habit and gorgeous fall color.

In October, the green summer foliage changes color from top to bottom in all shades of red from pink to deep burgundy. The red seed pods that open to reveal bright orange seeds persist after the leaves have dropped off. Birds eat the seeds although they are poisonous to humans. There are inconspicuous flowers in the spring.

Burning bush is easily propagated from suckers that grow up from the roots. You can dig these up and move them to another location. Also, semi-hardwood cuttings can be taken in early fall and easily rooted in the ground or in a pot. Semi-hardwood is the area along a branch where the new growth meets the old growth and is becoming woody and less pliable. The cuttings should have good roots in 6 to 8 weeks. Then they can be planted in a protected area or in a cold frame.

Growing burning bush from seed is a tricky business. If you take a seed apart, you'll see that under the orange covering there is a very hard white seed. Birds eat the seeds and this hard covering is somewhat broken down in their gullet then passed out and later germinated after alternately freezing and thawing in the ground. According to studies done at the University of Pennsylvania, the burning bush seeds will not germinate unless they pass through birds. They tried to soften the seeds with different acids and water treatments to get them to germinate, without success. There was a small success rate with detergent washings for four weeks then outdoor treatment for 15 months. Growing from cuttings is much easier.

Burning bush is generally free from pest and disease. Its cousin, winter creeper, *Euonymus fortunei* is often bothered by scale insects but burning bush, *Euonymus elata* is less susceptible. Scale looks like small brown or tan bumps on leaves and new stems. Spray with horticultural oil in fall or early spring if there is evidence of scale.

Fall Foliage

It's October on Cape Cod. The pageant of color in the garden is winding down before the time of winter rest. We don't get the feeling that we're moving through a bowl of "Trix" cereal "raspberry red, lemon yellow and orange orange" as in other parts of mapled New England. But we can enjoy our subtle landscape and create an autumnal vignette in our own yards with the flaming torch of one or two trees planted just for their fall foliage.

Here is a short list of trees with consistently good fall foliage. If you can't find one for planting now, ask your favorite garden center if they can order one for you to plant next spring. These trees are all hardy for our planting zone. Remember to give them plenty of space because they will all get very big.

To effect a golden glow with YELLOW fall foliage: Ginkgo - also called Maidenhair Tree. Beautiful fan shaped leaf. Try to buy a "male" tree. The female Ginkgo has malodorous fruit. Ginkgo does better with some lime added to Cape Cod soil. Leaves turn clear yellow in fall. Ancient adaptable tree around since the time of the dinosaurs.

<u>Honey Locust</u> - *Gleditsia triacanthos* - Look for cultivar called 'Sunburst' or 'Moraine' for thornless branches with nice open form. Drought tolerant. The new leaves in spring as well as the fall foliage are yellow. Add some lime to soil as well.

<u>Tulip Tree</u> - *Liriodendron tulipifera* - will get very tall. Has unusual shaped leaf that turns yellow in fall. There are large, pretty, tulip shaped flowers in late spring but they are often hard to see because they are at the top of the tree. Likes acid soil.

<u>Larch</u> - *Larix decidua* - This is a conifer whose needle-like leaves fall off in fall after turning yellow. The ones that grow wild along the highways in Northern New England (*Larix laricina*) will not do well here because our planting zone is too warm for them. The garden centers here have larch trees suitable for our zone.

For the RED family of fall foliage:
<u>Sourwood</u> - *Oxydendrum* - also called Sorrel tree. Bright red fall foliage with the added benefit of fragrant white flowers in drooping racemes. Ooh la la. Plant in full sun for best color. Likes Cape Cod soil.

<u>Sweet Gum</u> - *Liquidambar styraciflua* - looks like a maple tree with leaves that come to points at the tips,

but it is from a different family. Some have leaves that turn shades of purples, oranges and crimson. Has ball shaped fruit with a prickly covering that you don't want to step on with bare feet. Rake them up and save for dried arrangements. This is a beautiful specimen tree with pyramidal shape.

Zelkova - closely related to elms without the disease problems. Cultivar called 'Village Green' has wine red foliage in the fall. Will get very big.

Tupelo - *Nyssa sylvatica* - also called Black Gum. These grow wild in parts of Cape Cod, there are some beauties along Route 124 near Seymour and Long Ponds. Female trees have small dark blue fruit. Striking fall color in dark reds with some oranges mixed in.

Parrotia - This tree has it all. Might take a little phone time to find, but I've seen it at nurseries on Cape Cod. The leaves come out a reddish purple in the spring. Then they turn shiny green in summer. But the autumn is why we grow Persian Parrotia. The leaves turn many shades of red, yellow, orange, burgundy. And did I mention the exfoliating bark? Or the red flower stamens that stay on the plant all winter?

<u>Maples</u> - *Acer* - Maples are the obvious choice for fall color in the landscape. There are many varieties and cultivars from which to choose but they do have common problems that you will have to deal with. They have a shallow spreading root system that can rob nutrients from any surrounding plants. Subject to some pests and diseases, maples should not be allowed to get too dry for the first few years until they are well established to keep them strong and vigorous. A strong tree can resist pests and diseases better. But the fall color of many of the maples makes the extra attention worth it. <u>Acer griseum</u> - paperbark maple has beautiful cinnamon colored bark that peels. There are many <u>Japanese maples</u> with interesting leaves all season. <u>Acer rubrum</u> - the red maples are native to New England and have brilliant red fall foliage. Sugar maples, swamp maples, sycamore maple, so many maples!

So look around your property. Find a site that is sunny and suitable for a large specimen tree and set an autumnal bonfire with colorful fall foliage.

Paperwhites, Tools

For an easy project with spectacular results, how about forcing some paperwhite bulbs. 'Paperwhite' *narcissus* are originally from Africa and the warmer parts of Europe and Asia. They are considered to be "tender bulbs" which is another way to say, "if they freeze - they die". I know some people in Florida who think of themselves along those lines. The paperwhites have more hardy relatives, daffodils, that we can plant outside now for spring bloom. But don't plant the paperwhites outside, they wouldn't make it through the winter, even the mildest of Cape Cod winters.

Start out right when forcing paperwhites. Buy bulbs that feel solid and not mushy. Choose a container that does not have holes in the bottom because the bulbs need to be grown in either water or very damp potting mix. If you want to have them in a basket, use a solid liner. If you want to see the roots, use a clear container. You can use a deep or shallow vessel for paperwhites. If you use a very shallow container, the paperwhites might send out a lot of roots and push the bulbs right up and out of the pot. Ceramic bowls, old watering cans, glass pitchers, bread pans, you name it, these can all hold paperwhite bulbs.

Next, clean the container and fill part way with something that will hold the bulb up off the bottom so roots can come out. Some people use a layer of potting soil. You can also use glass marbles, small pebbles, white marble chips, beach glass, polished stones, and even glass eyeballs if you can find enough of them.

(Happy Halloween!)

Place the bulbs very close together, even touching each other, pointed side up. Paperwhites look good when grown in a large mass, so fill the container with as many as it will hold. Then surround the bulbs with the same filler as under the bulbs, but don't cover the tops of the bulbs.

Fill the container with water until it touches the bottom of the bulb. If you're using potting soil instead of pebbles make sure it is very damp. They should never be allowed to dry out until after bloom time. Place in a dark, cool area (frost free) for about a week: cellar, closet, under a table. This gives the roots time to form before sending up the leaf shoots. Then bring out to a bright location, on or near a window sill.

This should not be someplace too hot. Sometimes when the bulbs are kept too warm, they will only make leaves, no flowers.

In 2 to 4 weeks, Thanksgiving time, there will be very fragrant, Paperwhite flowers. If the leaves or flower stems seem like they are going to flop over, tie a ribbon or wire around the mass, half way up the stems. You also might want to try the cultivar 'Soleil d'Or' which have yellow flowers. After the bloom has gone by, discard the bulbs. The pebbles and other fillers can be washed and reused.

This is the time of year to get ready for winter storage of our garden tools. The tools will last much longer and perform better if we take care of them.

Have your lawn mower serviced over the winter instead of waiting for the spring rush. The Cape Cod soil (sand and salt) is particularly tough on our mowers. It can really beat up the blades. A worn out mower blade can break apart or get out of balance and cause engine problems.

If you want to do your own winter storage and maintenance of the mower, rototiller or gas edger, run them until the gas runs out. Take out the spark plug and put in a little oil, then replace the spark plug. If you want to change the engine oil in the fall, remember to refill it so you won't kill the mower when you start it next spring. It's okay to store over winter with oil in it.

Clean and sharpen your tools and then oil or spray with a lubricant that you can buy at the hardware stores. A sharp shovel works much better than a dull one. An easy way to oil a shovel is by keeping a bucket filled with sand and a little oil. After using the shovel in the garden, plunge it into the oiled sand a few times to clean and oil it all at once. Then remember to put it away out of the rain, and snow, and sleet, and hail.

As the perennials die back outside, we can find some of the hand tools that went missing when we left the garden to answer the phone last summer. These should be cleaned and sharpened too. I still haven't found my favorite claw or my best pocket knife!

November

Pumpkins

Halloween is over.. How many pumpkins do you have left over? I have four. How many are there still at the garden centers? Did you grow pumpkins this year? Have you ever been to the Harvest Fair at the Barnstable County Fairgrounds, or the Topsfield Fair? If you answered yes to the last question, did you see the entrants into the Giant Pumpkin Contest - the Sumo wrestlers of the plant world? I like tiny ornamental pumpkins as well as giant pumpkins; for the same reasons that I like both Bonsai miniatures and giant redwoods, for their superlative size.

Pumpkins are American plants. The name "pumpkin" comes from an old French term "pompion" for "cooked by the sun" or ripe. The botanical Latin family of the pumpkin is *Cucurbita*. It is closely related to other squashes, melons, and gourds.

Pumpkins are grown as annual plants in our climate. Their original source is a warmer place than Cape Cod and the plants will not winter over here. Given the right conditions, such as a nice warm compost bin, the pumpkin seeds can survive our winter and sprout the following spring. Pumpkins need a fair amount of warm weather and full sun to do well, but they can be grown successfully here. It is not a plant for the very small garden. The big leaves and trailing vines need room to spread.

When you're looking for pumpkin seed to sow next spring, there are many choices available including the unusual white one. The seed catalogue says that the white pumpkin should be harvested when slightly immature (August) because stress will cause a blue tinge to the skin. Blue and white pumpkins, what next?

Growing giant pumpkins has become a competitive sport. There are many pumpkin athletes here on Cape Cod. This requires special seed and remarkable techniques that sometimes take years to develop. There are even team entries into these contests. The festival where they are judged is at the end of September.

All pumpkins need full sun, well drained soil with plenty of moisture without being soggy. They are not too fussy about soil pH.

You can sow the seed directly in the ground or extend the season by starting seeds inside a few weeks earlier and plant outside when the first true leaves develop. Try not to disturb the tender new roots. They can be interplanted with a quick growing crop like radish or lettuce before the pumpkin vines get big.

We have some insect pests and wilt diseases that are spread by insects that can wipe out pumpkin hopes. Cover with spun polyester fabric until the blossoms are well formed to prevent the insects from boring into the stems and laying their eggs. Insecticides will not be able to reach the larvae of the squash vine borer inside the stems. The blossoms need to be pollinated by good insects or handy farmers with paintbrushes to get fruit, so remember to remove the row cover.

For home growers, harvest pumpkins when the shell is hard and fully colored. Leave several inches of stem on the pumpkin to extend the storage time (this goes for other squash as well). When you buy a pumpkin, look for one with a stem still on if you want it to last longer. The skins can harden up by being left outside for a couple of weeks after picking. When pumpkins are given the right conditions, (50 - 55° F with 70 - 75% humidity) they can be stored for a long time, from 2 to 5 months.

The term *pumpkin* is used for many different kinds of squash. The pumpkin pie filling that we buy might not be from an orange pumpkin at all. Pumpkins can be prepared for eating in numerous ways: as a soup, a vegetable side dish or main course, in bread, dried, steamed, fried, or pied.

Pumpkin seeds are a great snack food. They have long been popular in Mexican cooking as well. Just wash the seeds after scooping them out of the pumpkin, then bake on an oiled cookie sheet for about an hour at 250°. Shake the pan a few times during cooking and turn up the heat for the last five minutes to brown them a little. They can be salted or unsalted.

Pumpkins also make an attractive serving bowl when hollowed out. They can hold soup, dip, or a vegetable dish. The skin can have a shallow carving for more decorative display. Pumpkin cheesecake, pumpkin ice cream, pumpkin pudding, lots of kinds of pumpkin pies. Apples are originally from another continent. Someone should change the saying to, "as American as *Pumpkin* pie."

Late Fall Chores

There are still things to do for the garden in November. It's not winter nap time yet. If you haven't finished planting all the spring bulbs that you bought, don't despair, you can still get them in. The hardest part of planting bulbs is getting yourself out there to do it. The easiest way to plant bulbs is by digging a wide hole with a shovel and planting a group of bulbs at once, instead of one small hole, one small bulb. Forever!

While you're out there, a few other things to do: It's time to take the plastic tree wrap off the trunks of the trees. The purpose of tree wrap is to guard the trunks during transport from nursery to planting site. Once the tree is planted, the tree wrap can do more harm than good, and it should be removed. Studies have shown that tree wrap promotes damage by insect borers by giving them a perfect habitat. Also, dampness and extreme temperature changes under the wrap can cause bark problems.

Think of tree bark like skin and tree wrap like a plastic bandage. You know what your skin looks like when you leave a bandage on too long. Same with trees. The bark can split open and disease and pests can move on in. Young fruit trees might be an exception to this. If there is any evidence of rodent damage (chew marks) on the lower trunk, it should be wrapped for the winter and removed in the spring.

It's time to empty those window boxes. Pull out the annuals that have been killed by the frost and dump the soil onto the compost. Recycle the plants this way too if they were not diseased. After the window box is cleaned out, fill it with evergreen branches and colored berries such as bittersweet, pyracantha, holly, or winter-sweet. You can use some sand or clay to wedge the branches in the boxes so they won't fall out. This looks nice with autumnal displays too, using colored leaves and gourds.

If you have access to oak leaves, they make a great mulch for roses, rhododendrons and many perennials. Resist the urge to mulch until the soil beneath the surface is colder. A few more weeks probably. Oak leaves are good because they dry up on the trees before they fall to the ground.

Maples and many other leaves fall off the tree while they are still moist. They can mat down and smother plants when used as a mulch.

In the vegetable garden, this is a good time to cover the rhubarb patch with dried horse or cow manure. When the feathery asparagus greens are turning yellow, it's time to cut them off at ground level. We can still plant garlic for next year's harvest while the warm weather holds out. Plant garlic deeply (6 inches or so) to avoid rotting problems caused by freezing and thawing of soil near the surface. Yes you can use garlic from the grocery store for planting in the garden. Don't fertilize the garlic cloves in the soil until the spring.

For the indoor vegetable garden, you can take some left over cherry tomato seeds and plant them in a pot now. If you have a sunny window, you can grow cherry tomatoes inside the house for picking all winter. Indoor tomatoes need plenty of water and regular (weekly) fertilization. They can also be grown as a hanging plant for easy harvesting. Kids and salad makers think this is great! I knew someone in Maine who grew melons inside the house, against a sunny window. When the fruit got too large for the upright vines, she held the melons up with pantyhose and curtain rods. It was pretty funny. Cherry tomatoes and indoor herbs are more my speed.

Back outside, remember to feed the wild birds. Along with the seed you provide, birds eat the insect eggs that have just been deposited all over your property. These insect eggs hatch out into larvae that will devour your precious garden plants next spring. Wild birds come for water as well as seed if you can supply a birdbath with one of those heating devices that keeps it from freezing.

Don't forget to bring in the rosemary or sweet bay from the garden. Remember the canna, dahlia, glads, and begonias. They won't make it through the winter without your help. All right, maybe some of them will. Maybe we'll have another mild winter like last year. Don't plan on it. Remember all the snow from two years ago? Me neither.

Poison

The first seed catalogues for next year have arrived. By the end of January, we should have a nice big pile of them. The choices for plant material are always enormous. One of my favorite catalogues is from Thompson & Morgan (1-800-274-7333). I like it because it's free, has color photos of hundreds of plants, and it lists seeds for plants that I've never heard of and absolutely must try to grow.

The Thompson & Morgan catalog is using a new system of abbreviations and symbols for each plant listing. Among these symbols are three different signs for poison cautions. One is a little red cross for plants that may cause irritation to those with sensitive skin. Then there are two exclamation points in triangles: the red one means that this plant is toxic if eaten, the green one means it is harmful if eaten. A quick thumb through of the catalog shows that many of our common garden and house plants are potentially dangerous when handled incorrectly.

Serious poisoning from plants is relatively rare. According to the Poison Control Center, most plant poisonings involve children under three years old. They put everything in their mouth; berries, leaves, flowers, mushrooms, worms. My sister put a poisonous red berry up her nose when she was little and had to go to the emergency room to get it out.

Knowledge and prevention are the best ways to avoid accidental poisonings from plants. Learn what plants you have in your house and yard and which ones are poisonous. Proper identification is the key for this. The County extension office has a free list of common poisonous plants that they'll send to you. For a more comprehensive listing that includes pictures and descriptions, you can buy a *Peterson Field Guide* called, *Venomous Animals & Poisonous Plants*.

Poisonous plants can affect humans in many ways from the merely irritating to the lethal. Some have perfectly edible and deadly poisonous parts on the same plant.

Examples of this are:

rhubarb	-	poisonous leaves,
potato	-	all green parts of the plant,
tomato	-	leaves can cause blisters, and
apricots	-	most have poisonous seeds.

And just because you see a bird or animal eating a plant, it doesn't mean that it's safe for humans to eat. Birds eat poison ivy seeds. Deer and dogs eat everything.

The Poison Control Center gets calls according to the season. They just passed the busiest time for mushroom calls. Teach children early that the only mushrooms that can go in their mouth should come from the grocery store. There are some wild mushrooms that should not even be touched because the toxins can get on the hands and later put in the mouth. There are many attractively colored mushrooms growing all over Cape Cod in the fall. We have deadly poisonous mushrooms growing here too. One is even called " death cap".

Pretty soon, Poison Control will start getting calls about plants for holiday decorations. Poinsettias have a reputation as being highly poisonous, but there was only one questionable death in Hawaii in 1919 from eating this plant. Nevertheless, it is better to keep this plant away from children and pets, because it can make them sick even if it doesn't kill them. It is a member of the Euphorbia family. All the members of this plant family have a milky sap that can be irritating to the skin.

Holly berries can be poisonous when consumed in great amounts, but they are supposed to taste very bitter and it is unlikely that someone would eat very many.

Mistletoe berries, on the other hand can be toxic when eaten. There are good artificial mistletoe sprigs (extra kisses) for households with young children.

But even with our best intentions, accidents do happen, kids eat things they're not supposed to. If you have to call the Poison Control Center, their number is 1-800-682-9211, it's listed inside the cover of the phone book right under 9-1-1. They will ask for identification of the plant, which part was eaten, how much, and how long ago it happened. They will want to know the age and size of the person, and if they are showing any symptoms. It is important to act quickly because some plant poisoning symptoms do not appear for many hours, or sometimes days.

When you're ordering seeds this winter, remember that plant toxins can be most highly concentrated in roots and seeds. So make sure that children and pets don't eat your seeds when they arrive in the mail. Many of our garden flowers are harmful when eaten: daffodil, morning glory, sweet pea, delphinium. But that doesn't mean that we should stop growing them. I have to wear gloves when I work with the tomato plants because the leaves give me blisters, but I'll never stop planting them. Have a Happy Thanksgiving and keep those poisonous plants out of your mouth.

American Holly

If you want to walk off some of the turkey and pie, how about going to a place where you can see many beautiful holly trees. It's a bit of a drive from the lower Cape, but Ashumet Holly and Wildlife Sanctuary in East Falmouth is well worth it. This is a good time of year to view holly trees. The leaves have fallen off the deciduous trees and evergreens like the hollies stand out in the landscape.

Set on 49 acres with rolling hills and a pond, Ashumet Sanctuary has nice walking trails and over a thousand mature holly trees. There is a good crop of holly berries this year and you can see them in many colors at Ashumet - yellow, red, orange, black. The berries come in different shapes and sizes also.

The American Holly is native to Cape Cod. You can find them in wooded areas and old properties all over the Cape. Starting in the 1920's, Wilfred Wheeler, a skilled plantsman and the first Commissioner of

Agriculture for Massachusetts, began collecting specimens of the best native hollies from the Cape and Islands and other parts of New England. The collection was expanded to include outstanding English, Japanese, Chinese and hybrid hollies. They were then planted in a naturalistic setting at Ashumet Farm and managed by Wheeler and a man named Joseph Dias.

Mr. Wheeler became nationally known as the "Holly Man" which is not to be confused with the "Holy Man". He collected hollies and other more exotic trees and shrubs, for many years. The trees were propagated from cuttings or moved to Ashumet as whole trees. Many of the beautiful, tall holly trees at Ashumet are 60 to 100 or more years old. Ashumet Farm was donated to the Massachusetts Audubon Society in 1964 by Josiah K. Lilly, III, who had purchased it after Mr. Wheeler died.

"Ashumet" is a Wompanoag Indian word for "at or near a spring". Grassy Pond is the name of the spring fed kettle pond that is in the middle of Ashumet Sanctuary. The walking trails go all around and near the pond. You can walk for twenty minutes or hours. But leave the dogs and the clippers home. No pets and no cuttings allowed.

Large topiary birds greet you at the Ashumet Sanctuary parking lot. There is a great sign including Audubon maps and informative brochures about the trees and the wild birds, available at the trail entrance. The trail maps are not precise, but you can't get lost because you can usually see the pond, and all the trails intersect eventually. Ok, I got lost for a little while, but I did find the Franklinia tree and the Chinese hollies.

The Barnstable County Extension Service has a very informative, 10 page pamphlet available called, "Growing American Holly on Cape Cod". It was put together in the 1960's and 70's by Oscar Johnson who was the County Agent and Manager of the Cape Cod Extension Service. It was written in response to the many requests regarding the cultural practices for the American Holly. The Master Gardener hotline still gets a lot of calls every year about holly trees. The most common question is: "why doesn't my holly tree have berries?" It's probably a male.

The booklet covers the natural history of the American Holly *Ilex opaca* and its use as an ornamental landscape plant. There are also extensive directions and recommendations for soil requirements, planting, fertilizing, pest and disease control, pruning and propagation.

If you are interested in holly propagation, this is still a good time of year for cuttings (not at Ashumet nor in the National Seashore).

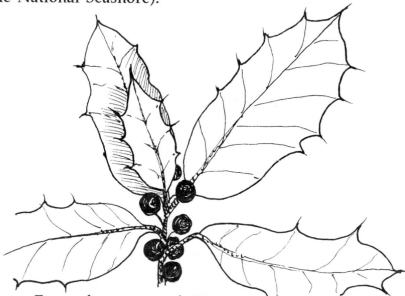

For a free copy of "Growing American Holly on Cape Cod", call the Extension Service office in Barnstable. The information-packed publication is designed to help the homeowner, the gardener and the nursery people. If you can find one at a nursery, you can still plant a holly tree at this time of year. Then next year, after Thanksgiving, maybe you can look out the window and see a red cardinal sitting on a branch of the evergreen holly tree. Perfect!

December

Christmas Cactus

I t is known as Thanksgiving cactus, Zygo cactus, Christmas cactus, Claw cactus, Crab cactus, and botanical Latin cactus names as well. But whatever you want to call it, this is a good choice for a flowering houseplant. If you provide a few simple cultural requirements, this succulent can live for many years. An heirloom plant.

The scientific names of plants are always being reviewed. The purpose of using scientific names (usually, but not always Latin) is to have a uniform base to identify plants for communication between botanists and regular ol' plants people of all nationalities. The current botanical nomenclature for Christmas Cactus is *Schlumbergera* with another name after that to further describe it like: *truncata* or *bridgesii*. It was named after Frederick Schlumberger (1805-1865) who was a Belgian horticulturist, explorer and plant collector.

No matter what the name tag says at the greenhouse store, the Christmas cactus is easy to recognize by both the unique foliage and flower shape.

The foliage is flat and grown in scalloped sections that are linked together in sausage fashion. The leaves form branches that become somewhat woody with age. There are sharp looking edges, but this kind of cactus has no spines. The blossoms are formed at the ends of the leaf branches which have a natural droop, so it is a good choice for a hanging plant.

Christmas cactus is classified as an epiphyte, which means it grows on another plant. This is not a desert cactus. It grows in the tropical forests of places like Brazil, on trunks and branches of trees rather than on the jungle floor. There are many tropical orchids that grow this way too. Bring your Christmas cactus outside for the summer, but keep it out of direct sunlight. It prefers filtered sunlight outside and full sun indoors, the same way it grows under the canopy of the Brazilian forest.

Christmas cactus has been hybridized for many generations to increase and improve flower colors and size. The wild plants usually have scarlet flowers. I read somewhere that they've been hybridized to produce yellow flowers. I've never seen one with flowers that color, have you?

For the long botanical word of the week, how about *thermophotoperiodic* ? Christmas cactus plants are thermophotoperiodic.

In everyday language it means that the flowering depends on temperature and light. Christmas cactus needs shortened day length and temps of 50° - 70°F for it to produce blossoms. If it gets too hot or too cold, it won't make flowers. Or if it gets too many hours of light, including indoor artificial light, it won't produce as many flowers if at all.

To get Christmas cactus to flower, start about three months before flowering time. Then reduce watering to a minimum. Keep the night temperature at 50°- 55° and the day temperature below 70°. This should initiate flowering regardless of day length. If you can't maintain these specific temperatures, you can induce flowering by controlling light hours. Give it good bright light for eleven hours only and don't let the temperature go over 70° or the buds may drop off. If you have a Christmas cactus that's been flowering every year for a long time, don't change anything except maybe an occasional repotting.

You can buy ready-made cactus potting soil, or you can make your own. Here's a recipe: combine 1/4 coarse sand, 1/4 peat moss and 1/2 potting soil. For every gallon of the preceding mixture add: 1 pint small gravel, 1 cup charcoal chips, 1 cup ground limestone, and 1 cup dried cow manure. Mix and let sit for a few days before using.

You can buy the gravel and charcoal at pet supply stores in the fish department. If you use this mix, you don't have to fertilize, and you don't have to repot for a couple of years.

Christmas cactus is generally not affected by insect pests unless it is severely stressed. If it is in a good location try not to move it around too much. This can cause bud drop - probably because of the changes in light and temperature. If the foliage is discolored, it is probably caused by either overwatering or nutrient deficiency, fertilize sparingly. If the leaves are faded, it's probably not getting enough light. If the leaves shrivel and get limp, it probably has a wilt disease. This is usually caused by overwatering. There's not much you can do to bring a plant back once it gets wilt diseases. Better to start with a new one.

It is an easy plant to propagate. Cut off some pieces of forked stems (a few inches long) from a healthy plant, and put them in potting mix. Keep slightly moist and you'll get roots in no time. You can try your own cross pollination to get flowers in a different color. If you come across a Christmas cactus with yellow flowers, let me know.

Tips and Trees

We lived in northern Maine for most of the 1980's. If we looked out the front of our house, we saw the United States, if we looked out the back we could see Canada. Gardening there was different than here on Cape Cod. It was not unusual to still have tulips on the 4th of July.

November was tipping time in Maine. The locals all had their favorite tippin' places where they'd go to cut the tips of balsam fir branches for making wreaths. This was how many families made extra money for the holidays. After filling their trucks and cars with balsam fir tips, they would make the wreaths using a metal ring and wire. Hard work, low pay. There were collection places all over the county where the wreaths were bought then trucked South. Maybe even to Cape Cod.

When the time came for getting a Christmas tree in Maine, we didn't go to the parking lot and buy one. We went out in the woods and cut one down. Moosehorn National Wildlife Refuge near Cobscook

Bay which is at the 45th parallel - the exact midpoint between the equator and the North Pole, used to open every December to let people cut one tree per family. Or some years we'd cut a tree from a friend's land. One year there was so much snow, we had to use the snowshoes and pull our daughter and the dog on a sled. But we got a great tree. Since we moved to Cape Cod we haven't used the snowshoes much, but they look good hanging in the garage.

You can get in a heap of trouble if you go out tipping or cutting in the woods on Cape Cod without permission. But you can take cuttings from a variety of evergreen plants on your own property to combine for a beautiful wreath or swag. The garden centers, florists and hardware stores have supplies for this.

The tradition of a decorated Christmas tree in the U.S. dates back to the time of the Revolutionary war when it was introduced by German immigrants. Before that, trees, wreaths and garlands had been a symbolic custom of the ancient Egyptians, Chinese and Hebrews although I don't think they used balsam firs. From pagan worship to various Christian religions, in Europe and Scandinavia, the decorated evergreen has a long history. After a longtime and widespread tradition in Germany, the Christmas tree became popularized in Victorian England and the United States.

Today, selecting the perfect Christmas tree has become a seasonal highlight for many Americans. Practically all species of evergreens are used as Christmas trees. The first choice to make is between artificial, live and cut trees. Those silver and pink metallic artificial trees aren't my favorite, but there are some very natural looking artificial trees available. Live potted trees are available for attentive indoor use with later outdoor planting. Buy these at your favorite garden center where you'll get good advice on the care and planting. Cut trees are available at practically every parking lot and garden center on the Cape.

There are some cut-your-own tree farms on the Cape in South Dennis, Mashpee, Forestdale, Barnstable and Falmouth. For these locations you can call the Barnstable County Extension office.

Freshness is important when selecting your tree. The needles should be resilient, not brittle. Run your fingers down a branch to make sure the needles adhere to the twigs. Shake or bounce the tree once or twice on the ground to make sure the needles don't fall off. If a few come off that's okay. Most of the parking lot trees were cut months back but they can still be good if you are selective.

Check the tree for fragrance and don't believe it when they tell you that the Christmas tree smell will get stronger when you get it inside. If the tree doesn't smell like balsam fir outside it won't in your living room either.

The longer the tree is indoors, the more combustible it will become. Be sure the tree is well supported in the base. You can use some fish line or string to attach it to a wall in a safe upright position away from heaters, televisions, fireplaces and other sources of heat. You don't want the fire department to come to your house for a Christmas tree mishap. Check the water level every day. They take up a lot of water in a dry house.

When you buy your wreath this year, think about all those Mainers out tippin' in the woods so they can buy the latest "hot" toy for their kids too.

212

Spices

It's holiday baking time again. Time to get out the spices that accent and enhance our culinary concoctions. The three spices in my cabinet that get the most use are ginger, nutmeg and cinnamon. If you ask, most people would say that spices are just ground up, powdery stuff in tins that come from the grocery store. Before they made their way to the food store and your table, spices came from plants. From bark. From seeds. From roots.

The quest for flavor has changed the destinies of nations. In the 1400's, Columbus followed the prime directive to search out the shortest route to the lands of the spices. At one time, cinnamon was of greater value than gold, "oooh, a cinnamon ring, thanks, Honey!" It was the most profitable spice in the trade of the Dutch East India Company. Nutmeg has been the subject of political plotting to keep its inflated price high.

Peppercorns have been used as currency. Ginger is an ancient Oriental medicinal plant that has also been used for food and perfume.

Cinnamon comes from the dried inner bark of a shrubby evergreen tree that is native to India, Australia and parts of South America. It was used as an ingredient for embalming in ancient Egypt and part of religious rites in medieval Europe. *Cinnamomum zeylanicum* is in the Laurel Family of botanical classification, and is related to the bay and sassafras trees. The cinnamon spice comes from the dried inner bark of the tree. The shoots are cut off close to the ground and harvested during the wet season in India and similar places. Then the outer bark is scraped away and the inner bark is peeled in layers to be dried as cinnamon sticks or pulverized into powder.

The cinnamon tree can be grown as an ornamental houseplant. It has large, shiny green leaves with attractive veining. The new growth of the leaves is red. Or you can try growing its close relative, *Cinnamomum camphora*. This makes a good indoor plant with glossy pale green leaves that emit a "Vicks vap-o-rub" odor when they are pinched. Both these plants are available through mail order from Logee's Greenhouses in Connecticut.

For a free catalog that includes Logee's extensive collection of rare plants, call 860-774-8038, or write them at 141 North Street, Danielson, CT 06239.

Nutmeg is the common name for the seed of the tree called *Myristica fragrans*. It is a long lived tree that can grow up to 65 feet tall. Too big for use as a house plant. Originally from Southeast Asia, it is widely grown as a commercial tree in many tropical areas including the Caribbean islands. Slow to yield fruit (8 or more years) it is at prime fruiting at 25 years and can bear for 60 years or longer. If you must have nutmeg for a houseplant, try growing nutmeg scented geraniums that are available from Logee's.

The fruit from the nutmeg tree resembles an apricot or an oval plum. It can also be round or pear shaped. When fully ripe, the gold or orange fleshy outer part of the fruit bursts open to reveal a brown seed that is covered by a crimson colored net which is called an aril or arillus. This aril is easily separated from the seed then flattened, dried and ground into a powder called Mace which has a lighter, milder nutmeg flavor.

The brown seed covering from inside the fruit is dried in the sun for 6 to 8 weeks and turned twice daily. The drying is finished when the seed inside shrinks away from the hard outer shell and rattles when shaken.

Then the shell is broken open and the nutmeg seed is picked out. Ground nutmeg looses its flavor more quickly than whole seeds. Buy the whole seeds and grind them as needed with the smallest section of your grater or get a nutmeg grater from a kitchen shop.

Ginger comes from the herbaceous perennial or biennial called *Zingiber officinale*. It is also native to tropical Asia but has been carried all over world and grows in just about all places that don't freeze. The aromatic, pungent rhizome (fleshy underground stem) is dried and ground, peeled and preserved, or used fresh.

It can be grown as a houseplant if you can provide consistent warm temperatures (around 75° F.). Try growing it from the ginger roots that are available at the grocery store. They need a big pot because the stems and leaves get about 3 feet tall and the rhizome gets quite big. It is slow to germinate so be patient. Keep the potting soil moist but not soaking or the ginger will rot. Fertilize once a week when you start to see shoots and leaves. When grown this way, there is often no flowering, but it still makes a beautiful plant and you can harvest fresh ginger root at any time. Then you can make everything from ginger candy to ginger brandy.

After the Holidays

he calendar says it's winter? The temperature outside is 53° and I just planted the last of the spring flowering bulbs. As a master gardener for the Extension Service, I do not recommend that you wait until the end of December to plant spring bulbs. But as a busy procrastinator, I say anytime you can get that hand spade in the soil, it's a good enough time to plant spring bulbs.

When you're outside, you might notice some broken, criss-crossing or diseased branches on your trees and shrubs. Regardless of the season, it's always a good time for maintenance pruning. Here's an old proverb that I just made up - "it's foolish to wait when you can prudently prune today".

There are a few pruning rules that are in effect all year long; use proper tools and keep them sharp and clean. Dull pruning tools can rip, crush or tear the bark and branches, and they are much tougher on your hands and arms. You can buy some terrific hand-tool sharpeners that fit in your pocket.

Dirty pruning tools can spread disease from one plant to another. Wipe them off frequently and dip them in a bleach and water solution.

For most homeowners, if you have to get up on a ladder to do some pruning, call a professional tree person. Not just any lawnmower guy, someone who has some tree education, someone who knows what *arborculture* means. Save the new chainsaw for cutting firewood on the ground. If you want to do your own high pruning, try using the cutters that come with pole extensions rather than using a ladder. All right, if you really insist on going up that tree, remember these three important numbers when climbing up the ladder: nine, one, one.

New Years Eve is coming right up. If fresh flowers are going to be a part of your party decorating, there are a few tips that can help you make the most of arrangements. Most flowers should be retrimmed at the base to help them absorb water better. Cool water temperatures will prolong the life of cut flowers. If you buy flowers that are still in bud and you want them to open more, put the stems in warm water for a few hours then back into cool water. I've seen florists be quite rough with flower buds, flicking them, peeling down the petals and even tapping the buds on the table tops to get them to open. Warm water seems less brutal.

Water is an unnatural medium for most flowers (other than water lilies). The plants decay and decompose when the pores fill with water. To slow down this process, remove all the leaves that are under water, in a vase. It is recommended that the water be changed frequently, every day, or every few days if you use those little pouches of flower food. This can be bothersome if you made a nice arrangement and you don't want to start all over each day. Place the vase with the arrangement intact right under the kitchen or bath faucet and let cool water run until it is up over the sides and completely exchanged.

If you use soaked oasis or florist's foam (green porous material) the arrangement will be supported better, but it will probably not last as long as it will in water. Flower stems should be inserted by holding the stems at the bottom and feeding them slowly into the oasis. If you hold them high or up near the blossom and push, the stems can buckle or break. Then you have to cut them off and have a short stemmed, "I did that on purpose, isn't it sophisticated" arrangement.

Remove the flowers as they turn brown, take some of the left over pruned stems or evergreen branches from your yard and add them to the display.

You can combine many disparate objects with intriguing shapes and colors to make your arrangements unique. Add pretty fruit or vegetables.   Spray paint some branches. Wash something off that you got at the swap shop and place it in a vase with fresh flowers.

While everyone is admiring your arrangements at the party, you can think about what you're going to make for your New Year's resolution. My list includes: finally getting that water garden going, and work on being a more gooder writer.

Index

Index

Index

To order additional copies of Out In The Garden,
please complete the information below.

Ship to: (please print)
           Name: _____
           Address: _____
                        _____
                        _____
           Day Phone: _____

____ copies of Out In The Garden @ $12.95 each _____
postage and handling @ $2.00 per book _____
MA residents add 5% tax _____
Total amount enclosed _____

Make checks payable to: *Invisible Ink Publishing*
Send to: 2 Smith Lane
Brewster, MA 02631

- -

To order additional copies of Out In The Garden,
please complete the information below.

Ship to: (please print)
           Name: _____
          .Address: _____
                        _____
                        _____
           Day Phone: _____

____ copies of Out In The Garden @ $12.95 each _____
postage and handling @ $2.00 per book _____
MA residents add 5% tax _____
Total amount enclosed _____

Make checks payable to: *Invisible Ink Publishing*
Send to: 2 Smith Lane
Brewster, MA 02631